domino

THE BOOK *of* DECORATING

domino

THE BOOK *of* DECORATING

a room-by-room guide to creating a home that makes you happy

Deborah Needleman
Sara Ruffin Costello & Dara Caponigro

Produced by

 MELCHER MEDIA

Published by

SIMON & SCHUSTER

New York   London   Toronto   Sydney

Published by
Simon & Schuster, Inc.
1230 Avenue of the Americas New York, NY 10020

First Simon & Schuster hardcover edition October 2008

SIMON & SCHUSTER and colophon are registered
trademarks of Simon & Schuster, Inc.

For information regarding special discounts for bulk purchases, please contact Simon & Schuster Special Sales
at 1-800-456-6798 or business@simonandschuster.com

Produced by
MELCHER MEDIA, 124 West 13th Street, New York, NY 10011.
www.melcher.com

Printed in China
10 9 8 7 6

Library of Congress Cataloging-in-Publication Data
Needleman, Deborah.
Domino : the book of decorating : a room-by-room guide to creating a home that makes you happy /
Deborah Needleman, Sara Ruffin Costello, Dara Caponigro.
p. cm.
1. Interior decoration--Handbooks, manuals, etc. I. Ruffin Costello, Sara. II. Caponigro, Dara. III.
Domino (Condé Nast Publications) IV. Title. V. Title: Book of decorating.
NK2115.N34 2008
747—dc22   2008015072

ISBN—13: 978-1-4165-7546-7
ISBN—10: 1-4165-7546-4

Cover art: de Gournay wallpaper pattern "Portobello" on dyed silk.
www.degournay.com

for the lovely and talented staff of *domino*

table of contents

introduction 8

CHAPTER 1 **getting started** 11

CHAPTER 2 **the entryway** 25
STORY OF AN ENTRYWAY: *Rita Konig*

CHAPTER 3 **the living room** 51
STORY OF A LIVING ROOM: *Deborah Needleman*

CHAPTER 4 **the dining room** 83
STORY OF A DINING ROOM: *Lili Diallo*

CHAPTER 5 **the kitchen** 109
STORY OF A KITCHEN: *Sara Ruffin Costello*

CHAPTER 6 **the bedroom** 135
STORY OF A BEDROOM: *Kirsten Hilgendorf*

CHAPTER 7 **the bathroom** 163
STORY OF A BATHROOM: *Chase Booth*

CHAPTER 8 **the office** 187
STORY OF AN OFFICE: *Dara Caponigro*

CHAPTER 9 **the kids' room** 213
STORY OF A KID'S ROOM: *Ruthie Sommers*

the decorators' handbook 239
A guide to window treatments and upholstery

the big black book 251
A guide to the best decorating resources

acknowledgements 265

introduction

When we started *domino* in 2005, my fellow editors and I began with a straightforward and somewhat naïve goal: to demystify and democratize decorating.

In my fleeting attempts to decorate the places in which my family lived—a series of Manhattan apartments and a ramshackle weekend house in the Hudson Valley—I'd encountered the obstacles familiar to many of our readers. Simply choosing which sofa to buy was complicated enough, and getting wallpaper nearly impossible. I couldn't even gain entrance to the arcane temples known as design showrooms, which were open only "to the trade." The familiar shelter magazines, including the one where I'd worked for several years, were filled with "aspirational" homes: strikingly beautiful fantasies, with little relation to the way I lived or anything resembling a budget I could afford. I wanted my home to make me happy. But the route there seemed designed to frustrate me.

We were convinced that decorating didn't have to be a mystery, a burden or an additional source of anxiety in our busy lives. As I say, we were a bit naïve. We thought all we had to do was explain the decorating process, share secrets from the professionals we most admired and bust a few antiquated cartels. What we discovered along the way was that we had to do something more than gain direct access to the wallpaper supply. We had to create an alternative route for our readers, who faced the same decorating quandaries we did: How can you decorate without making unnecessary, costly and time-consuming mistakes? How can you produce a result that reflects who you are, how you live—and perhaps even the image you want to convey?

This book reflects everything my co-authors and I have learned about answering those questions. Connoisseurs say that looking, looking and more looking is the key to learning about anything visual, whether it's great rooms, gardens, art or architecture. But over the years, I've found that I can understand a subject more readily and appreciate it more deeply when I have some context—a base of knowledge—on which to ground my thoughts while I look. So that's how we organized the book.

We decode pictures of spaces we love in order to show how to "read" a room (*Great Rooms and Why They Work*). We break rooms down into their components to illustrate how they can be "layered" piece by piece (*Building a Room*) and also arm you with the need-to-know facts we wish someone had given us. We share the insights we've garnered from the homes we've been lucky enough to visit (*Ideas to Steal*). And finally we reveal the stories behind how our own rooms came into being (*The Domino Effect*)—because, of course, real life is messier and less linear than any manual.

Just three years after we started, decorating is a lot more democratic than it used to be. If you consult the back of this book, you'll find that "civilians" have more access to resources and insider tricks than ever before. I'd like to think that our magazine has played a role in that transformation. But more than that, I hope this book reflects the spirit that has guided us—the joy of finding your own style and creating a home that is about the way you choose to live.

Happy decorating!

Deborah

Deborah Needleman

getting started

1. find inspiration

CAST A WIDE NET in looking for ideas. Magazines and books—decorating and otherwise—are natural starting points, but movies, art, fashion, nature and travel are also rich resources. Don't think about it too much—just grab what you love: Tear out or copy pages, save images from the Internet, gather photos and postcards (being sure to mark the specific attributes you love for future reference). Be literal—collect paint chips from the hardware store—and be populist: A matchbook in the right color can be every bit as useful as a photo of Jackie O's boudoir. Don't be shy about including fantasies: You might not get to replicate that palace ballroom, but a picture of it could supply a solution or help shape your aesthetic.

START A FILE of these favorite things. Depending on how you like to organize, you can use a basket, an accordion folder, a bulletin board or a binder, or you can save in an online file (like "My Deco File" on dominomag .com). It can be as high- or low-tech as you like: The best system is the one you'll actually use.

LOOK FOR THEMES in the images you've compiled. After you've spent some time amassing, take stock. Have you picked several things that feature the same yellow? Lots of gilding? African-esque patterns? Are you drawn to rooms filled with stuff or ones that are more spartan? Get a little ruthless now with your images and ask yourself: "Do I really love this? Does this merit keeping?"

THE WELL-LIVED LIFE
YVES AND MICHELLE HALARD

CAPTURED ON FILM BY THEIR SON, FRANÇOIS HALARD,
TWO OF FRANCE'S GREAT DECORATORS ENJOY THE
RESULTS OF A LIFETIME OF COLLECTING IN THEIR
DISTINCTIVE HOUSE IN THE SOUTH OF FRANCE

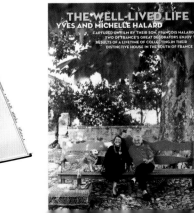

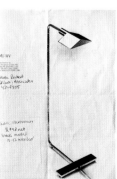

2. determine your style

Gather all the threads you've identified, and try to attach words to them. Don't worry about settling on one term; people tend to have a style that's mostly this with a little bit of that: kind of bohemian plus a dash of classic, mostly Dorothy Draper with a dollop of Sid Vicious. It might seem like a parlor game, but naming your style really helps you focus and filter out the things that don't fit and pinpoint those that do. It makes it easier to answer the question "Is this me?" as you flip through a catalog or face down a chair in a store. You see the trendy chair and think, "It's cute but I'm going to get tired of it because I'm more into tailored classics," and then you walk away—money saved and mistake averted.

bohemian *feminine*
elegant *vibrant*
masculine **clean**
tailored organic
classic **traditional**
modern
exuberant **bold**
unconventional
sentimental *witty*
comfortable **punk**
ladylike edgy cozy
zen romantic **noir**
dramatic pop

classic and neutral
but also a little bohemian

theatrical, unconventional
yet spare and modern

laid-back, glamorous and
traditional, but with a twist

3. consider how you'll use the room

THINK ABOUT YOUR LIFESTYLE and decorate accordingly. Being honest about how you live is essential to creating great spaces. Practical needs, not just style aspirations, should guide your plans. You may fantasize about a formal living room where you can hold fancy parties, but if a) you don't entertain all that much, and b) you end up with a setup that doesn't accommodate the things you or your family enjoy, like watching movies, then someone's going to be unhappy. Bear in mind that a room that looks like a showroom also feels like one, and nobody will want to set foot in it (and there's nothing sadder than an unused room).

OBSERVE WHAT DOESN'T WORK in your current scheme, and strategize about possible fixes. Do you never listen to music because your speakers are in the wrong room? Do you resent the too-small coffee table when guests come over? Addressing the failures and hassles allows you to create a room that benefits you, as opposed to one that dictates how you live.

How many people do you need to seat?
Will the room be for entertaining, for family or both?
Do you have children? Pets? Is it more of a daytime or nighttime space?
Will it function as a formal parlor or more like a den? Do you want to be able to put your feet up on the coffee table?
What activities will happen here?
Work? Art projects? TV watching?
Do you want to hide your TV?

4. assess your stuff

PHOTOGRAPH everything (yes, everything!) in your home—furniture, rugs, lamps, art—and lay out the images. Seeing each piece in isolation gives you distance and makes it easier to decide whether it passes your style filter. (Photos also make it simpler to envision new schemes because you can "move" things from room to room.)

SORT your pictures into four groups: keep, change (paint, reupholster), give away and sell. Take a good hard look at each item you've photographed and ask yourself, "Do I love this? Do I need this? Does it fit with what I'm trying to create? Is it my style?" Be tough in determining what works in your life. If you've hung onto Grandpa's desk for 10 years but could never stand the sight of it, you're not going to start loving it tomorrow. So let it go. Unless something is beyond repair, donate it or give it away on freecycle.org rather than putting it in the trash.

MEASURE all the things you're keeping so you'll know exactly what can work where when you're devising floor plans.

Empty cabinet, paint it red and move to the kitchen.

Love these—find a spot for them!

Reupholster with brighter fabric.

Time to bite the bullet and buy a flat-screen.

Coffee table too big for sofa—find replacement.

Donate!

5. draw up a floor plan

LOOK AT THE BONES OF THE ROOM and decide what to highlight (e.g., a fireplace) and what to hide (radiators). Also, think about how the room will appear when you walk in. For example, some people don't like seeing the back of a sofa.

SELECT TOOLS to simplify the job. You can use graph paper and pencils, make life-size paper templates of furniture to move around in the actual space or find tools online (icovia.com has a handy drag-and-drop program). Whichever method you choose, bear in mind that all guides are rough and that furniture in two dimensions always feels smaller than it looks in three.

MAP OUT OPTIONS rather than trying to find one perfect solution. Every plan involves compromise, but if you spend some time considering a few arrangements, you'll find one that's best for you. Remember the importance of function and that composition and style go hand in hand. If your look is formal, you'll be happier with a traditional sofa plus a pair of armchairs rather than a more offbeat layout.

one room, three ways

fireplace as focal point

Comfortable and built to foster conversation, this closed, symmetrical layout has a more buttoned-up feel, though it's made up of modern pieces. A so-so view of the TV makes it clear this is definitely a living room, not a den.

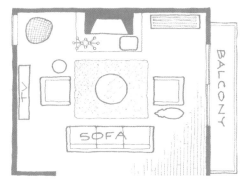

all eyes on the TV

With the sofa positioned to face the screen and big pillows scattered on the floor, this casual layout is good for movie nights (or marathon TV sessions) and is especially cozy for children (or adults who don't mind sprawling on the floor).

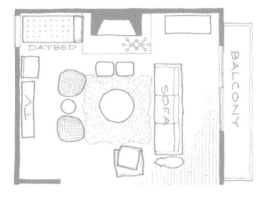

ideal for entertaining

Turning the sofa to face the view and positioning a low daybed opposite keep the sight lines to the window clear and set the stage for mingling: Traffic easily flows to and from the balcony; the daybed makes a perfect group perch.

6. set a budget

FIGURE OUT WHAT YOU HAVE TO SPEND and be realistic about
how much things cost. Many people will drop $300 on a pair of shoes but balk at the same
price for a side table guaranteed to last much longer. If you're renovating, remember that
it almost always costs more than you think it will and can easily consume your entire
renovating and decorating budget. It pays to be conservative and factor in a buffer, so
you'll have enough money left for decorating afterward.

CHOOSE AN APPROACH that meshes with your personality. Impatient types
might want to do the entire space at once, even if that means using less expensive pieces.
More tortoise-like characters are happy collecting slowly over time. And some people like to
splurge on one major element that eats most of their funds, leaving them to just keep what
they have or go totally cheap on new additions.

MAKE A SHOPPING LIST that allocates the money you've got among the stuff
you need. Use this list to track what you should spend versus what you actually do spend,
so you can stay on budget.

LIVING ROOM BUDGET

	ESTIMATED	ACTUAL
sofa	1,500	
side chair	600	
console	400	
coffee table	700	
curtain fabric	1,500	
rug	600	
pair of lamps	700	
floor lamp	500	
TOTAL BUDGET	6,500	

do the whole space at once

If you're up for devising a master plan and carrying it out, figure out the cost of the big-ticket item (for instance, the draperies here) and then divide the rest of your budget among what's left to buy.

collect slowly over time

Locating the pieces of your dreams can take a while, but sometimes doing without for a stretch is preferable to settling for second best. If you spent a mint on dining chairs, it's okay to eat in the kitchen until you can afford that just-right table.

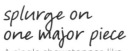

splurge on one major piece

A single showstopper, like this statement-making wallpaper, can completely transform a room.

7. research, research, research

Once you have an idea of what you are looking for, investigate what's out there in your price range. It pays to educate yourself and shop around. Pound the pavement, check out design blogs and post questions on their forums, talk to friends about their favorite sources and buy a bunch of magazines to familiarize yourself with resources. Begin to gather your finds—paint and fabric swatches, catalog clippings, printouts of online items—in a file or box.

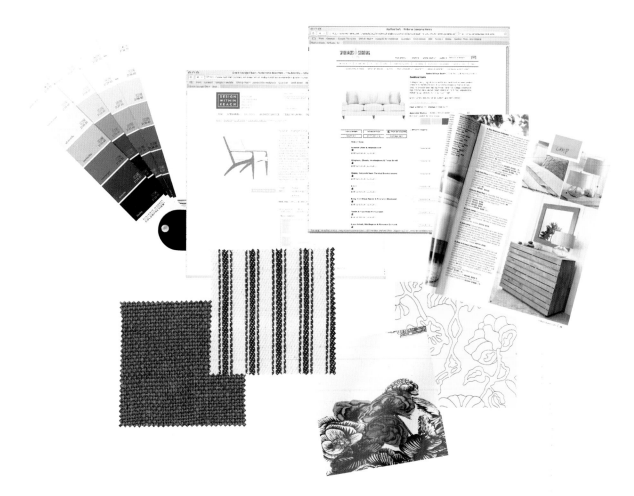

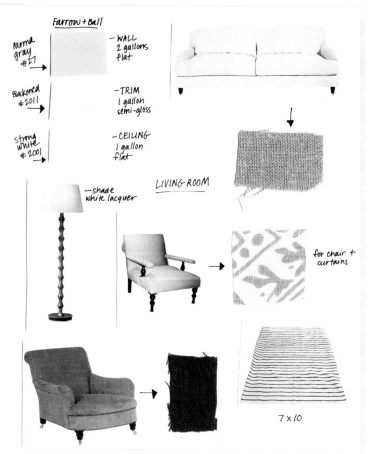

Farrow + Ball

parma gray #27 → — WALL 2 gallons flat

Blackened #2011 — TRIM 1 gallon semi-gloss

strong white #2001 — CEILING 1 gallon flat

— shade white lacquer

LIVING ROOM

for chair + curtains

7 x 10

8. create a design scheme

This transitional step between planning and doing is all about narrowing down your options and seeing how everything looks together. It's hard—both to make decisions and to factor in practical considerations—but like doing a puzzle, it's also fun and creative.

CONSOLIDATE the information you've amassed. Pull together your floor plan, your list of things you need, pieces you're keeping and/or changing, images of favorite items, fabrics and paints, and the size of your budget. Factor in limitations (e.g., this rug is available only in these three colors).

SEE HOW YOUR CHOICES STACK UP TOGETHER. If you're set on a neutral sofa, those beige paint chips might go out the window and the blues you selected might become keepers. If it turns out all your chairs are really leggy, your best sofa bet might be the one with the skirt, which offers a little balance.

9. make a decorating schedule

Even if you're not a to-do-list person, you'll want to take this final step because it saves so much time and cuts way down on confusion. Draw up a list of everything that needs to be done and be specific: Order this sofa, order this fabric for throw pillows, buy two gallons of this paint, hire a painter, send this chair to the upholsterer. Breaking a project down into steps reminds you that you don't have to do it all at once, makes very clear what needs to be done and keeps the process from feeling overwhelming—all of which will help you carry it through to completion.

- Order paint. (Confirm with painter when he will be coming.)

- Order sofa in pale natural linen. Make sure to specify with skirt.

- Order 2 club chairs in navy solid.

- Order occasional chair. Send them fabric.

- Make appt. with local decorating shop to discuss making curtains. (Take my domino book with me!)

- Call antique shop and see if I can take floor lamp out on approval.

- Order 7 x 10 striped rug.

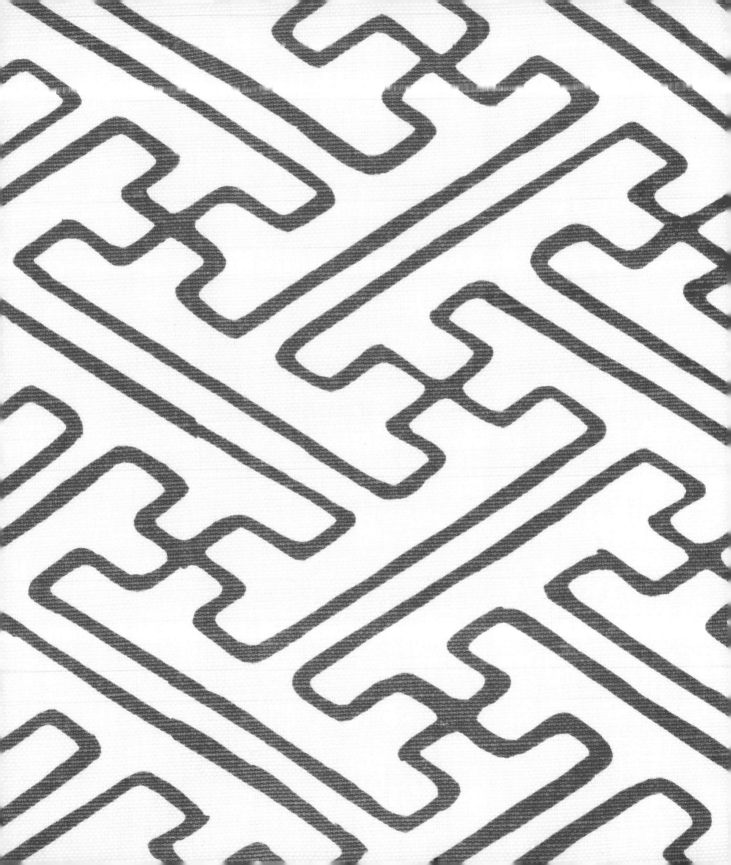

CHAPTER TWO

the entryway

the style.
happy graphic

VIVID POPS OF COLOR White walls and an ebony floor create a flexible backdrop for Crayola-bright accents—an orange side table and primary-colored accessories that give the area its peppy personality (but could easily be switched out for a whole different palette and mood).

DIVIDED BUT CONNECTED A see-through folding screen creates an entry where there isn't actually one, while also allowing sunlight to filter in. The half-in, half-out zebra-printed cowhide rug links the entry to the rest of the apartment.

LIGHT AND AIRY Uncluttered open shelves and the simple fretwork of the screen ensure the space has ample room to breathe. Even the giant mirror contributes to the sense of expansiveness with its delicate, peacock-y detailing.

FRIENDLY FORMS The furniture plan is very casual—no serious pieces, no imposing symmetry. All the elements are pleasantly askew, except for the centered mirror, which creates a sight line and holds everything together.

Fashion designer
Liz Lange's
entryway, decorated
by Jonathan Adler

the style:
brave bohemian

GUTSY SPECTRUM The teal entry hall (with red pendant lamp—
nearly its opposite on the color wheel) and the bold hues leading off from it
work together because they are all equally rich. White trim offers a breather
between them.

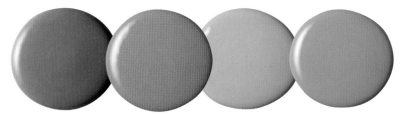

COLOR AS A MASK The nook may be unremarkable architecturally,
but it feels confident and considered, thanks to the daring paint application,
which graciously hides the flaws. Painting over mismatched molding and
unappealing pipes allows them to recede from view, while the red pendant
draws attention up and away from the drab floor.

OFFBEAT SENSIBILITY There is a flea-market magic to the
combination of a Venetian mirror, an industrial-looking lamp and a
chinoiserie chest against a saturated backdrop. Leaning the mirror, as opposed
to mounting it on the wall, enhances the vignette's casualness, as does the tiny
picture hung off-center.

Entryway of
James Leland Day,
stylist

the style.
cool collector

WHITE LINING Epoxy floors and stark walls create a gallery-like setting for art, sculptural chairs and a mahogany chest, allowing the individual pieces to stand out. As full as the room is, there is a certain lightness accentuated by chrome, gilding, Plexiglas and the reflective floor finish.

UNEXPECTED FURNITURE Instead of a console or bench, a classic dresser anchors the space. It feels sober and historic, balancing the more playful elements like the mix of colors in the art and the 18th-century grotto chairs. The black picture frames and lamp shade pick up on the dark wood chest to tie things together.

DEVIL-MAY-CARE ATTITUDE A column of art hung behind the door from ceiling to floor feels informal and proclaims its unconventionality. Strings of beads draped loosely atop the lamp shade, the messy stack of books on the chair and even the missing knob from a drawer signal a laid-back demeanor. On the chest, little toys mingled with a fancy gilded frame are a final stroke of bad-boy behavior.

Entryway of Johnson Hartig,
fashion designer

the big piece: consoles, chests and benches

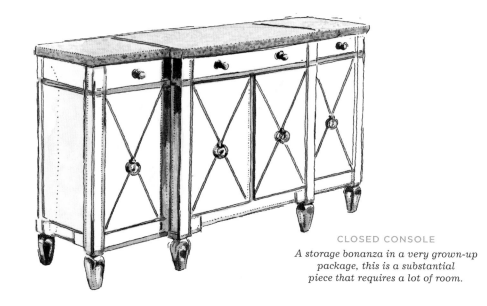

CLOSED CONSOLE

A storage bonanza in a very grown-up package, this is a substantial piece that requires a lot of room.

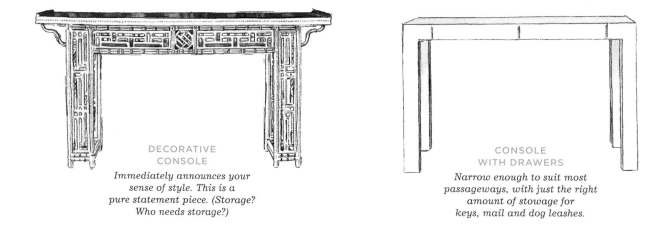

DECORATIVE CONSOLE

Immediately announces your sense of style. This is a pure statement piece. (Storage? Who needs storage?)

CONSOLE WITH DRAWERS

Narrow enough to suit most passageways, with just the right amount of stowage for keys, mail and dog leashes.

BENCH

Used as a drop zone for bags or a perch for taking off or putting on shoes, this can be accessorized with hooks installed overhead and baskets underneath if closet space is lacking.

CHEST

Not for cramped quarters (be mindful of its depth), this looks very homey topped with a pair of lamps. Readily holds both current needs and out-of-season gear.

OPEN SHELVES

A slender profile that won't bulk up a small space. Slip baskets onto the shelves to create additional storage.

DEMILUNE TABLE

Semicircular with delicate legs, this graceful option has a formal, old-fashioned feel. It offers minimal storage, but an easy-to-navigate shape (no corners to bang into!) makes it perfect for tight spots.

CENTER

Classic, graceful. Tends to be more formal. If you have a big enough entryway, this is often the best solution, floating or centered in the space. Can double as a dining table in a pinch.

INSTANT EXPERT:
buying an entry table

SIZE The length of consoles varies, but the height (30" to 32" is standard) and depth (about 14") are fairly consistent.

PLACEMENT Position the piece so it's a focal point as you walk into your home—whether that means it's front and center or off to one side (ideally not behind the door). Clearance is important: There should be enough space not just for the door to open but for a person to enter comfortably.

how to mix and match

gilded bamboo

'80s decadence

earthy fibers

parisian glamour

ornately eastern

scaled-up kasbah

storied refinement

minimalist mirror

flashy floral

why these pieces work together

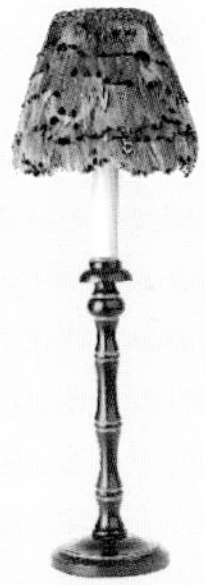

feather-capped diva

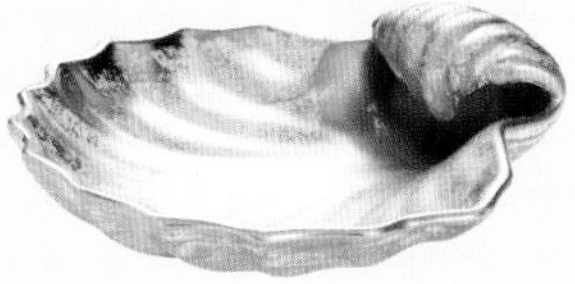

golden bowl

Bold, blingy and decorative, this rich collection trumpets **Park Avenue fabulousness**. Gold accents unite high-end pieces, including a very traditional candlestick lamp with an eccentric pheasant-feather shade. A simple natural-fiber rug keeps the glitz in check, and a gilded shell bowl bridges the showy and the organic.

translucent pyramid

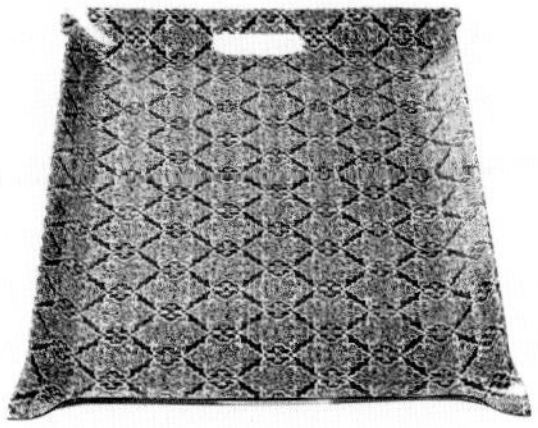

glossy tray

This **modern Moroccan** group marries exotic embellishment—a fanciful mother-of-pearl mirror and a graphic rug—with contemporary materials such as the translucent lamp and the laminated tray. A mirrored finish relates the 1930s cabinet to the shiny elements on the mirror and lamp.

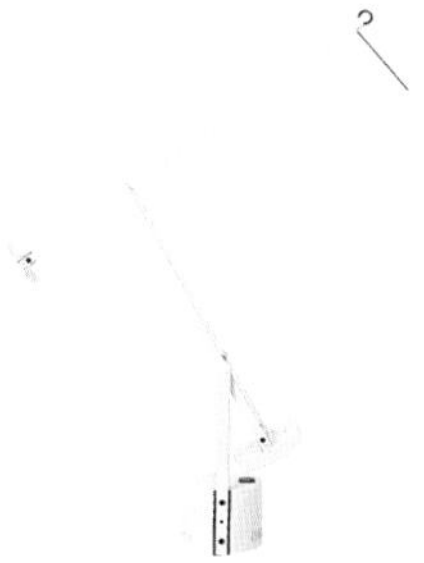

high tech

'70s mod

An unusual blend of the past and the modern age, this **futuristic neoclassical** mix is united by a crisp palette and an elegance of form. The rug—a blown-up riff on a standard floral—connects the intricate table with the streamlined tray, lamp and mirror.

very important tips

function & style

A TWO-TIMING SPACE Your entry is a way station, but it's also the mood-setter for your home, so practical and design concerns need equal attention.

SET THE SCENE Fresh flowers, neat tabletop compositions and dimmers on your light sources (or low-wattage bulbs) help create a pleasant atmosphere. Because the entry is where first impressions are made, it's an ideal place for a scent, whether you prefer a candle, incense or a diffuser.

MAKE IT WORK FOR YOU Establishing designated spots for the things you deposit or pick up as you go in or out cuts down on chaos. Use a tray to corral essentials like keys, cell phones, wallets and sunglasses; add a bowl for coins; hang hooks or get a coatrack to keep scarves, coats, hats and bags at the ready (and off the floor or table). An umbrella stand can also hold sports gear, and a wastepaper basket lets you toss junk mail as soon as it arrives: Once it fills, just transfer to the recycling bin.

lighting & mirrors

TABLE LAMPS If you have the space, a lamp or two on a console bestows a welcoming glow. No room for lamps? Go for sconces.

OVERHEAD FIXTURES A pendant lamp or chandelier in the entry offers major impact. Hang it at least 7' from the floor (so nobody gets hit on the head) and clear of the door.

DIMMERS Putting light sources on a dimmer lets you control the brightness depending on the situation (bright for reading mail, low for parties).

MIRRORS When in doubt, go big: A grand mirror makes a dramatic focal point. Match the frame to your table for a pulled-together look, or mix things up. If you find a mirror you like but aren't sure about it, ask to take it home on approval, a request many dealers are happy to accommodate. If nothing in the stores seems right, consider custom. At a good frame shop, you can choose the exact size, frame and type of glass (antiqued, tony-looking beveled, plain). This option is not necessarily cheap but yields exactly what you want and is a great way to copy an unaffordable antique.

storage

COAT CLOSET Little additions will help you make the most of the space. A basket for each family member enables everyone to find his or her stuff in a hurry. Low hooks on the back of the door allow children to hang their own coats. Matching wooden hangers are the easiest way to keep bulky coats in order; those with a thin profile save room but are still sturdier than plastic. If possible, shift off-season outerwear to another spot in your house, so the hall closet isn't jammed. It makes hosting (and even hanging your own coat) a much more gracious experience.

NO COAT CLOSET Opt for a piece of furniture with ample storage, such as a chest or a closed console. Choose hooks or a standing rack that works with the main piece. If you use individual hooks, mount them far enough apart so coats drape nicely (and consider installing them in a slightly out-of-sight spot, like behind the front door). Turn the major piece of furniture into a de facto closet by giving every area of it a purpose—fit it with drawer organizers (ideally in the top drawer) for smaller items, as well as dividers (in the lower ones), either giving each family member a space or grouping items by type.

floors

RUG SIZE Furniture is typically set off the rug in an entryway—but beyond that, there aren't many rules for floor coverings. A rug that takes up most of the floor space helps the area feel more like a room, a runner is good for a narrow corridor and a border (see above) adds definition, but it's also perfectly acceptable to go rugless.

RUG DURABILITY For this high-traffic zone, choose something flat (so the door can open over it) that can handle a lot of traffic. Sea grass isn't particularly durable, but it's inexpensive and works in any setting. Well-made antique rugs can usually take quite a beating (and likely already have).

PAINT INSTEAD Painted floors are an easy, low-maintenance option (you can sweep or mop them). If you're inspired, stencil a pattern or stripes (be sure to seal the surface after it's thoroughly dry). Since the entry is a contained area, it's a good spot to try something fun.

decorating tricks

CEILING-MOUNTED CURTAINS flanking a doorway add drama to the act of entering the house and also keep out drafts.

A TUNNEL OF EXUBERANT WALLPAPER is an exciting lead-in to a serene living room.

ONE BOLD WALL framed with grosgrain ribbon is a bright way to say "Come in."

FAKE A STAIR RUNNER—and the decorative border—with glossy paint.

A CHEERFUL STENCILED FLOOR is a playful alternative to an entry rug.

more decorating tricks

CREATE ARCHITECTURE by introducing molding to walls and doors.

INTENSELY PATTERNED WALLPAPER can be a surprisingly unifying backdrop for disparate pieces of art.

ONE GIANT PHOTO anchors a sea of smaller ones and makes an event out of a blank space.

DRESS UP OPEN STAIRS with patterned carpet to turn basic steps into something luxe.

ONE REPEATED MOTIF lining a hallway is intriguing and original.

small-space solutions

A NONSPACE MAXED OUT with standout pendants, over-the-top wallpaper and vividly painted doors becomes an attention-getting entry.

ESTABLISH AN ENTRYWAY with a chest and a chair placed near the door.

RIG UP A VESTIBULE that eases the transition from outside to inside.

CARVE OUT A "COAT CLOSET" with wall-to-wall hooks and baskets for hats and gloves.

SCONCES FREE UP SURFACE AREA in a petite foyer, leaving room for favorite objects.

finishing touches

DECKING OUT AN ENTRY with a punchy umbrella stand, a pretty tray for keys and a basket for newspapers makes staying organized more pleasurable.

HUNG TIGHTLY, an assemblage of art and mementos feels full and leads the eye up the stairs.

A BASIC POTTED PLANT is a low-maintenance but equally lovely alternative to flowers.

DRAWER DIVIDERS in this desk allow it to function like a clutter-free command center: leash, envelopes, stamps—check!

COMPOSING A TABLEAU with beautiful objects makes it even nicer to come home.

the domino effect

the starting point

"The tiny entry hall in my equally tiny one-bedroom is a space I wanted to give some importance to."

RITA KONIG
domino *contributing editor*

"An entrance should smell good because scent is the first thing you respond to when you walk in a house."

"I don't usually like overheads, but this metal light on a long chain makes my lofty ceiling feel more intimate."

dark elements

my inspiration

"This is Odorantes, a little flower shop in Paris. They prop the place with a rotating collection of taxidermy—woodland animals, butterflies, birds. The walls are dark, and all the colors of the flowers just pop against them. I went there for a *domino* story, and I couldn't stop thinking about it."

"I brought my mother [decorator Nina Campbell] to Odorantes, and she was so taken with the birds and the black of the shop that she designed this wallpaper. It was perfect for my entry."

"To highlight the wallpaper, I painted the door and everything around it black— even the doorbell."

"The hats are here because they take up a lot of space in the closet, and they fit nicely here."

"I don't smoke, but this ashtray has stayed with me through every apartment I've had. I just adore the color. I saw it in an antiques shop with my mother, and she bought it for me as a gift."

"I love a lamp illuminating something like a vase of flowers, giving it some weird prominence, as if it's on a stage."

finishing touches

"I wasn't sure about this, but I brought it home to try and it worked beautifully."

"I like small pictures propped against the wall—it's so easy to switch up the art."

"When I added the table and lamp, suddenly my sliver of a hall became a room."

major pieces

my entryway

"The lovely thing about wallpaper in an entry is that it gives the feeling that the space goes on and on—continuing beyond what you can see—whereas with paint your eye stops at the edges." —RITA KONIG

CHAPTER THREE

the living room

the style:
edgy classic

HISTORIC HUES WITH A TWIST A Colonial robin's-egg blue is rendered in a brighter shade, pulling it out of its old-fashioned shell. The pea-green fabric on the curtains and daybed complement the blue, while acid-yellow pillows—a riff on formal Georgian yellow—are a punchy grace note. The painted ceiling creates a sense of being wrapped in color.

WALLS/CEILING   CURTAINS/DAYBED   PILLOWS

MODERN MOMENTS The room is dotted with bygone accents—a brass library lamp, the crystal chandelier—but the central element is a clean-lined daybed, which bridges casual and formal. The bare floor, uncommon in a traditional living room, enhances the unfussy feel.

PROPORTION PLAY The mingling of grand and small pieces infuses the space with a lively rhythm. The curtains, the tall mirror and the bust on the stand add height to the low seating.

OFF-KILTER SYMMETRY A pair of chairs placed at a diagonal help tie the room's two seating areas together. Asymmetry pops up around the mantel, where frames are staggered rather than perfectly aligned. Even the tilted hat on the bust shakes things up—it says the room doesn't take itself too seriously. Like the overall mix, it's a relaxed take on classicism.

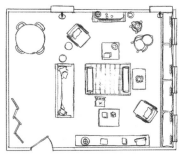

floor plan
This layout is all about maximizing seating. A double-wide daybed divides the large space into separate areas—one oriented toward the fireplace for entertaining, the other side for TV-viewing. A banquette offers yet more places to sit.

Living room of Sara Ruffin
Costello, *domino creative director*

the style: earthy modern

TEXTURED NEUTRALS This is not cold-lined modernism. The all-white backdrop is a stage for warm hues represented by diverse materials—cowhide, wood, leather, wool and cashmere. Silver accents bring some sparkle to the brown-and-white scheme.

WALLS · SOFA · SOFA · RUG

LOW FURNITURE The whole room happens below the windows, creating a lounge-y atmosphere. Short bookcases draw the eye horizontally and feel just right in relation to the close-to-the-ground coffee table, which signals casual, on-the-floor hanging out.

SCULPTURAL LIGHTING In lieu of standard table lamps, moonlike lanterns and an arced floor lamp add to the sense that the room is all abstract forms.

GEOMETRIC ASSEMBLAGES While the sofas aren't the same height, they work back-to-back, thanks to side tables that balance the composition. The TV is a focal point of the room, but surrounded by similar rectangular shapes (the art around it and the open shelves beneath), its central position is minimized.

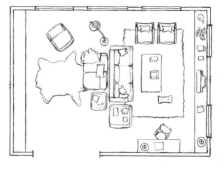

floor plan

Sofas divide this big space into two sitting areas—an open one that faces a wall of floor-to-ceiling bookcases and another centered around the TV. Nonmatching rugs help define each area.

Living room of Derek and
Michelle Sanders, *architect
and fashion director*

the style:
mid-century elegant

GLAMMED-UP BEIGE The secret here: neutrals played up by sumptuous fabrics and hits of icy blue, which add polish to the camel tones. A push-pull dynamic between cool (blue pillows, pewter curtains) and warm (gilt mirror and coffee table) makes the space both serene and inviting.

ICONIC PIECES Classic designs, both modern and traditional, appear in a mélange of textures: the thin paper of the Noguchi lamp, the smooth leather of the Arne Jacobsen chair, the wood of the Richard Schultz side table and the plush velvet of the Billy Baldwin sofa.

LADYLIKE DETAILS Shiny silk curtains, satiny pillows and floral fabrics contribute a subtle layer of femininity.

TOUCH OF ANTIQUE A gracefully time-worn mirror and round coffee table (an excellent foil to a boxy seating area) introduce some history and patina to the modern mix. The photographic seascape is a cheeky stand-in for a formal oil painting, its placement charmingly unexpected.

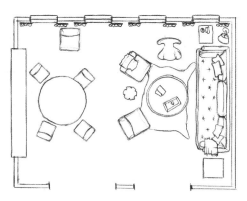

floor plan

A rug defines the sitting area in this loftlike all-purpose room, which is open to the dining area and a wall of bookcases. The furniture arrangement is easy and comfortable for socializing—an intimate spin on a formal setup.

Living room of model
Haylynn Cohen, decorated
by David Lawrence

the style:
cultured
irreverence

STRANGE BEDFELLOWS Contrast drives the room's punk-patrician effect. A gilt Louis XV sofa mingles with a '70s Bond-like chrome chair and crystal candleholders—wildly different styles, but they feel harmonious because they are all glamorous, decadent and a little rock and roll. The large see-through coffee table also helps unify—it's simple, so the other pieces can be outrageous.

POP COLORS Glossy floors and stark walls (offset by a rustic wood ceiling) provide a calming backdrop for a cornucopia of art in vivid hues.

CONTROLLED CHAOS The salon-style art assemblage could feel unwieldy, but strict framing and hanging (pictures line up precisely around a dominant central work) yield a sense of happy order.

EXAGGERATED PROPORTIONS In Lucite, the massive table doesn't overwhelm. Its scale is cleverly mirrored by the giant Damien Hirst spin-art painting.

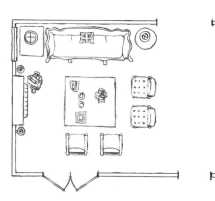

floor plan
Situated to the right of the front door, the living room functions as an entry hall (a chest and two chairs make up the actual entry). The formality and symmetrical arrangement of the furniture signal that this is not a comfy den but a salon.

Living room of Johnson
Hartig, *fashion designer*

the big piece: sofas

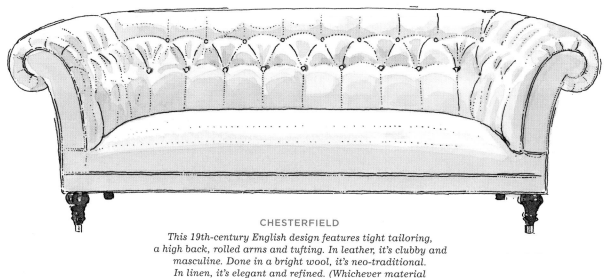

CHESTERFIELD

*This 19th-century English design features tight tailoring,
a high back, rolled arms and tufting. In leather, it's clubby and
masculine. Done in a bright wool, it's neo-traditional.
In linen, it's elegant and refined. (Whichever material
you choose, make it a solid.)*

CAMELBACK

*Dating back to 18th-century British designer
Thomas Chippendale, this piece has an
old-world sophistication but also looks surprisingly
modern in a solid linen. Hand-me-downs
can be updated with a tailored slipcover.*

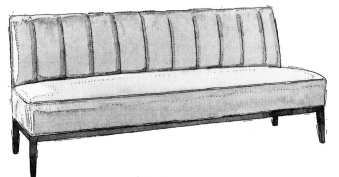

SLIPPER

*Streamlined and unfussy, like an elongated
slipper chair, this option is made more for
entertaining than lounging. Usually lean and
open, it does well in small spaces.*

TUXEDO

A signature of society decorator Billy Baldwin, this sofa is luxurious yet decidedly no-frills. A straight profile (the arms and back are the same height) give it a more masculine feel. Works in any room, modern or traditional.

FRENCH SETTEE

Often seen in a Louis XIV style, this regal option is delicate, formal and architectural. The exposed carved-wood frame provides a structured contrast in a room of heavily upholstered pieces.

ENGLISH THREE-SEATER

Rumpled yet aristocratic, this British country-house staple has soft, deep cushions and low arms that make it ideal for TV watching.

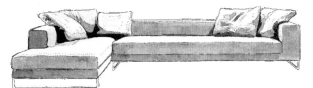

SECTIONAL

Casual, with a '70s lounginess. Good for establishing a sitting area in a loft. Minimizes need for other seating. A version with legs cuts the bulkiness.

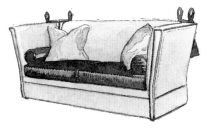

KNOLE

Named after a grand house of King Henry VIII. Super-classic and formal but very cozy and sheltering. Hinged sides untie and drop flat, so you can lie down.

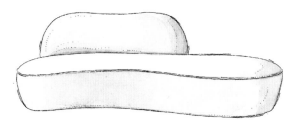

MODERN

More sculpture than sofa (this one is a mid-century design by Vladimir Kagan). Can float in the middle of a room.

INSTANT EXPERT: buying a sofa

WELL-STUFFED Knead the edges of the arms to see if a sofa is amply padded. It shouldn't be easy to detect the wood under the stuffing.

COMFORTABLE Test the seat depth (too deep can be awkward unless you like to sit with your legs curled up), the angle of the sofa back and the height of the arms.

FLAWLESS STITCHING Make sure the seams are straight and create a smooth, continuous line, without obvious zigzags, lumps or gaps.

STRONG FRAME Wood blocks in the bottom corners of the frame reinforce a sofa by dispersing weight. Feel underneath to check—not all sofas have them.

how to mix & match

streamlined modern

colorful kilim

classic gourd

properly skirted

floral indulgence

nature undercover

danish angularity

op art

animal magnetism

sculptural cube

rugged butterfly

There's nothing formal about this comfy, inviting setup built of browns and gray with a touch of red. A distressed-leather chair, a raw wood table and a handwoven rug paired with a slick sectional and a glossy lamp add up to a look that's **earthy yet urbane**.

lacquered curves

dazzling color

Ladylike tailoring and playful touches run throughout a mostly white lineup that's feminine but not at all princess-y. The cushy sofa and demure pillow are typical girl props, but the gold-lined lamp shade, mid-century-esque stool and grape-colored armchair take the decor a step beyond dutiful daughter.

pale minimalism

updated slipper

Rich textures—a ribbed rug, smooth black leather and cool marble—bring a sensual element to an **elegant, neutral collection** of largely modern shapes. The organic warmth of a pendant lamp made of antlers interrupts the strict geometry.

very important tips

coffee tables

SIZE The standard height is 17" to 19". Lower feels more modern. Length depends on the size of your space, but a good rule of thumb is to pick a table one-half to two-thirds the length of your sofa, so it's accessible from the entire sofa. Place the table about 18" away—within easy reach, yet leaving enough room for legs.

THE RIGHT SHAPE A square or rectangular design offers an orderly backdrop for decorative items, particularly books and trays. A shelf beneath can stash newspapers or remotes while keeping the top clean. Circular always looks neat because it's never crooked and is a good way to balance out hard-lined furniture. For a laid-back option, try an ottoman (a tray on top will make it functional), which can also double as seating.

SOLID OR TRANSPARENT A see-through table (glass or acrylic) can make a small room seem more spacious. A solid that matches the rug or floor (above) tends to disappear.

rugs

DIMENSIONS Standard rugs measure 6' x 9', 8' x 10' and 9' x 12'. Whether you go the standard or custom route, get one that leaves 4" to 8" of bare floor on all sides, so it looks intentional, rather than like imprecise wall-to-wall. Rugs with borders tend to be more traditional and are a nice way to lend polish to a room.

RULE-BREAKERS Conventional wisdom says all four legs of the sofa should be on or off the rug, but if you're buying a standard-size rug and the math just doesn't work out, don't panic—having two legs on is also okay.

COLOR & PATTERN A rug that brings in all the colors of the room can pull a space together; a patterned rug is often used to offset a scheme full of solids (above). But don't feel compelled to introduce a pattern—sometimes a textured solid rug can add all the interest you need.

LAYERING Throwing a smaller rug over a larger one (particularly of sisal or sea grass) helps define an area, like the spot where the coffee table sits.

window treatments

SHADES OR CURTAINS Curtains add drama and soften a stark space. Shades (like the roman ones above), are tailored and neat, and especially good for smaller spaces. You can match the style and fabric of your curtains to your room to play up what's already there or use them as a counterpoint. Sheers bring a fancy room down a notch, while formal drapes dress up understated furniture.

CURTAIN STYLES Lined curtains are weighty and rich, and feel formal. Unlined are breezier.

BEYOND ROLLER BLINDS If you want some glamour without a lot of bulk, try a lush hybrid like a roman shade or a swankier London shade (has a swag of fabric at the bottom). If you stick with a basic roller, you can elevate it with a border or trim, like pom-poms or tassels.

MOUNTING An inside mount (above) gives a crisp look and is especially nice with attractive woodwork. An outside mount for shades can make the window appear bigger. With curtains, hanging the rod higher and wider than the frame has the same effect.

lighting

LAMPS The easiest way to pull together a living room is to place a pair of matching lamps symmetrically on end tables or behind the sofa. For a looser but still unified feel, split a pair—one on an end table and one on a desk.

HANGING FIXTURES A chandelier in the living room is a nice surprise, adding elegance and dimension. You need a minimum ceiling height of 9', and hanging the chandelier over the coffee table ensures people won't bump their heads.

MIXED SOURCES A combination of table and floor lamps allows you to distribute light more evenly around a room (a matched set plus one floor lamp is a good starting point). Ditch the overheads if you can—they cast a harsh light.

WHERE TO PUT LIGHTS Make sure there are good lamps by reading chairs. Use smaller lamps to create a glow in unlikely places, such as on a mantel or a bookshelf.

decorating tricks

A BLAST OF COLOR in an elegant black-and-white scheme makes a potentially intimidating space friendly.

POUFS DO EVERYTHING— they're extra seating, footstools and even coffee-table stand-ins.

ONE SPECTACULAR PIECE with scale and drama is like an exclamation point in a room.

GRANNY UPHOLSTERY feels fresh on a sofa with modern lines.

USE YOUR RUG AS INSPIRATION for your overall palette—just borrow the colors for paint, furniture and accessories.

more decorating tricks

A TABLE THAT HOVERS just off the floor invites guests to sit on the rug and hang out.

HIDE AN UGLY SOFA with a piece of linen or another weighty fabric that pools a bit on the floor.

FRAMED WALLPAPER is an affordable way to bring in an expensive pattern.

A BAR TRAY conveys old-fashioned hospitality. You don't need a special piece of furniture—any tiny table will work.

GIANT HOUSEPLANTS lend regal symmetry and drama to a neutral space.

more decorating tricks

LAYER FLATWEAVE RUGS
that share the same basic
palette for a kasbah effect.

A SINGLE UPHOLSTERED WALL in a warm print softens stark furniture and stands in for art.

TWO COFFEE TABLES, instead of one, shake up the monotony of the living-room suite.

DIFFERENT-COLORED CURTAINS add theatricality to a space with high ceilings.

PAINT A BORDER to give character and depth to a room that has no molding.

small-space solutions

A HEADBOARD BECOMES A MINI WALL between living room and sleeping area in a studio apartment.

CLEVERLY PLACED ART can distract from messy storage.

SKIPPING THE COFFEE TABLE can make an undersize living room feel airier.

LET THE BED BE THE CENTER OF ATTENTION—no need to apologize for living in a studio!

CREATE A ROOM DIVIDER out of a backless bookshelf, giving privacy to the bed without blocking light to the interior.

hanging artwork

A HUGE PIECE, CENTRALLY LOCATED on the wall, anchors any arrangement. No matter how randomly you lay out the smaller ones, it looks considered.

DIFFERENT COLOR FRAMES prevent a geometric grouping of like pieces from feeling static.

OVERSIZE AND HUNG LOW, simple images can become the focal point of a room.

ONE VERTICAL, ONE HORIZONTAL—in a pair of intriguing graphic frames, it almost doesn't matter what's inside them.

AN ARTFUL GRID turns personal photos into poetry.

arranging a mantel

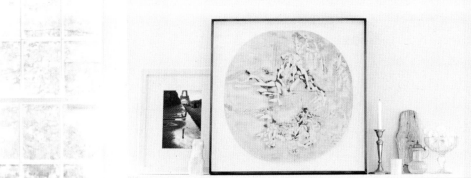

IN A MONOCHROMATIC STILL
LIFE, varying materials and
textures keeps things interesting.

A JUMBLE OF FAMILY PHOTOS lightens up an orchestrated mantel.

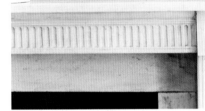

TUCKING A SMALLER ELEMENT behind a major mirror adds a layer of intrigue.

UNIFIED TONE PLUS ONE COLOR—a basic strategy that always works.

BRIGHT VASES AND UNUSUAL FLOWERS invigorate the symmetrical mantel recipe.

the domino effect

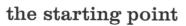

the starting point

"I wanted the living room in our loft to do two things I hoped weren't contradictory: function as an elegant, grown-up space for entertaining and be welcoming for my children."

DEBORAH NEEDLEMAN
domino *editor in chief*

major anxiety: my sofa

"I was completely paralyzed: What if I bought one and hated it? I decided a classic Billy Baldwin sofa was safe: It could add a little glamour if I wanted to go modern or clean lines to a more antique-y room."

my inspirations

"I'm always drawn to faded, subtle colors over bright, clear primaries. I prefer creams and ivories to whites, and I love chalky grays."

"Filled with a spot-on mix of styles, *domino* Editor at Large Tom Delavan's house is spare, sexy and comfortable. There's not a lot of color, but it's enveloping and warm and full of interest."

"This Brooklyn town house—which was kind of grand but totally cozy in that charming English-aristo way—had this rich, medieval-looking velvet I totally fell for."

stuff I ditched

"I've never been comfortable with anything too of-the-moment. So goodbye to my trendy missteps—a flokati rug, a Philippe Starck chair and Mercer Hotel–inspired dark bookshelves (which got a shiny coat of white paint)."

stuff I kept

"Everything I held on to felt a little timeless, handmade and collected: things I found in Stockholm with my husband, a modern Indian table I'd obsessed about for weeks, a French ticking pillow given to me by Dara Caponigro."

friend-erator to the rescue

"I couldn't quite pull it all together until I enlisted help. Tom Delavan chose furniture and fabric (like painted chairs and mousy-gray velvet) that would only look better as they got a little beat up."

"Tom also balanced my fussier pieces with more sculptural shapes and introduced modern elements, like giant paper lanterns and a Lucite coffee table."

my living room

"Coming home to a calm space makes me so happy and lets me take total pleasure in the wildness of my children. If the place felt or looked chaotic, I don't think I could love all the chaos it contains quite as much." —DEBORAH NEEDLEMAN

CHAPTER FOUR

the dining room

the style:
urbane organic

SOPHISTICATED NEUTRALS This basic brown-and-white palette is earthy but polished. Pickled-wood floors and pale Venetian-plaster walls add texture and make furniture seem to float.

CHAIRS SEAT
BACKS OF CHAIRS
WALLS

THOUGHTFUL PROPORTIONS Key sculptural elements anchor the room. The Noguchi paper lantern is large enough to serve as a focal point for the whole space, but it's also delicate, so it doesn't overpower the dining table. Similarly, the massive table feels light, thanks to its arched base.

ROUGH WITH REFINED Wicker storage baskets, industrial metal shelves and a raw wood ball play against the elegant mid-century dining table by T. H. Robsjohn-Gibbings and linen-upholstered Louis XVI chairs.

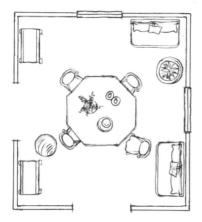

floor plan
The room has a lot going on—it's both TV den and dining room—but basic geometry keeps it from feeling busy. A pair of sectional sofas is split up into two corners and balanced by a pair of bookshelves, all of which surround the central table.

Dining room of
Dara Caponigro,
domino *style director*

the style:
ladylike luxe

FEMININE PALETTE All the colors in the scheme come from the wallpaper's pale blue, brown, silver and white. Contrast provided by the dark chairs and patterned pillows grounds the soft tones.

WALLPAPER CHAIRS SETTEE PILLOWS BENCH

FANCY AND FRIENDLY The seating is all aristocratic in style (Chippendale-style bench, Regency settee, Directoire chairs) but mismatched, for a cumulative effect that is offbeat and inviting. The sea-grass rug is casual (unlike a formal oriental), underscoring the idea that this is not an off-limits environment.

POSH ELEMENTS This room does not shy from sumptuousness. Cascades of silk taffeta pool on the floor; velvet upholstery (a thread that ties together the stylistically disparate seating) brings richness. Silver objects, a mirrored cabinet and a glass chandelier lend sparkle.

ALWAYS WELL-DRESSED With the good silver on display (and in use), the room looks perfectly accessorized all the time. Having something on the table keeps the mood welcoming.

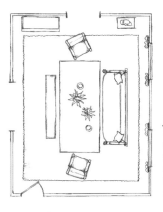

floor plan
In this funky layout, a traditional centered-table configuration is shaken up by unusual seating— a bench, a settee and armchairs that stand in for conventional dining chairs.

Dining room of
Windsor Smith,
interior designer

the style:
enchanted mod

SNOW-WHITE COLORS The juxtaposition of hues from nature (forest-y green, deep ocean blue) with icy walls and upholstery has a charming vividness.

| CURTAINS | CHAIRS | CHAIRS | WALLS |

DELICATE LINES From the Saarinen-esque table and leggy chairs to the wall-mounted bookshelf, everything seems weightless (even the curtains hover slightly above the ground). There's plenty of air around the furniture, which helps give the room its ethereal, otherworldly quality.

FAIRY-TALE SCALE Small furniture heightens the grandeur of the big, high-ceilinged space. Superlong curtains and a tall bookshelf further elevate the drama.

A DASH OF PIXIE DUST The starlike acrylic chandelier stunningly combines mid-century lines and magical ornament.

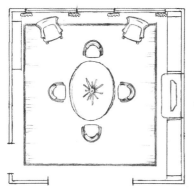

floor plan
Symmetry is the perfect nod to formal architecture—it makes sense to follow rather than fight the bones of a room. A classic arrangement here makes the modern pieces feel at home among grand proportions.

Dining room of
Fawn Galli,
interior decorator

the big piece: tables

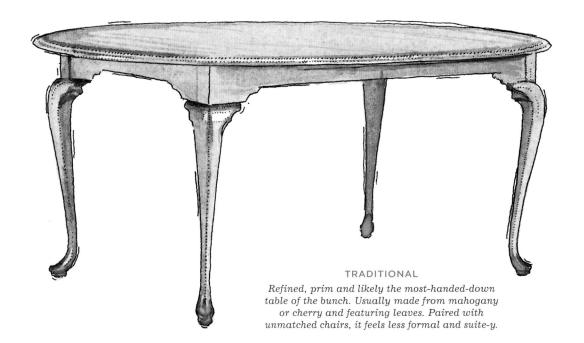

TRADITIONAL

*Refined, prim and likely the most-handed-down
table of the bunch. Usually made from mahogany
or cherry and featuring leaves. Paired with
unmatched chairs, it feels less formal and suite-y.*

TRADITIONAL PEDESTAL

*Dates to the Roman Empire and repopularized in
18th-century England. A round table is easy to sit at—
no legs to navigate. Can come with leaves, which
expand its surface into an oval.*

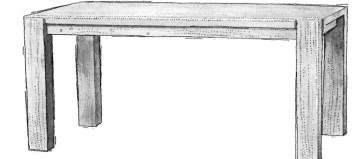

RUSTIC MODERN

*In a rough-hewn material, this is earthy,
spare and substantial. Warms
up a minimalist room, and its simple shape
guarantees it goes with any chair.*

MODERN PEDESTAL

Elegant, versatile mid-century classic designed by Eero Saarinen for Knoll. Takes any chair and complements any style room.

FARMHOUSE

Common in the 18th century, especially as a kitchen worktable. Rustic, with a laid-back country quality, this works well with modern chairs.

SWEDISH

Based on an 18th-century design inspired by French neoclassicism, this style is typically light and often casual in feel. Painted finishes give the look an unpretentious quality.

TRESTLE

Generally fabricated of a coarse wood that improves with wear, this form dates to the Middle Ages. Sitting at the ends can be a challenge.

INSTANT EXPERT: buying a table

SHAPE & MOOD
Round tables are great for group conversation. A more interesting alternative to one large rectangle is to try two smaller squares—use one for dinner with a smaller group, and push both together when you have a crowd.

STANDARD HEIGHT
Most tables are 29" to 30" high. If you find something lower that you like, be sure to pair it with similarly proportioned chairs so sitting and eating aren't uncomfortable.

HOW MANY PEOPLE FIT?
A 48"-diameter table seats four and can squeeze in six. A 54" table accommodates six comfortably; a 60" seats eight to ten. Standard size for a traditional rectangle for eight people is 36" x 72".

THE RIGHT SURFACE
Think about how you live and what you can tolerate: If stains and rings make you crazy, pick a piece that gets better with age—like a farmhouse table rather than an unsealed marble-topped one.

how to mix & match

tailored simplicity

glossy chippendale

opalescent brilliance

functional sculpture

parisian couture

modern art

sleek icon

playfully exotic

theatrical flourish

streamlined federal

greek key

Formal with subtle twists, this collection of **unstuffy classics** features traditional designs in unexpected materials or finishes—a chandelier strung with oyster shells instead of crystal, a chair in bright white rather than dark, polished wood—and a dramatic contrasting mix of dark and light.

urbane swagger

beige border

An elegant **1930s French** spirit infuses these compact elements just right for smaller spaces. Varied in texture, they bring together the warmth of camel (seen in the chair, table and plate) offset with white.

fiery statement

ethnic texture

A medley of patterns and multiple reds lends this group of youthful and **happy chinoiserie** pieces a distinctly modern bent. A clean white Saarinen table and ikat-embellished plates keep the look from veering off into a Chinatown theme park.

very important tips

chairs

HEIGHT Standard seat height is 18" (a table is 29" or 30"). Generally, you want your chair backs to be higher than the table. If you're going for a super-modern, low-back chair, make sure the back is at least table height.

COMFORT If the store allows, bring home a chair to test with your table before committing to a whole set. Have everyone in your household try it out. Upholstered chairs are usually more comfortable than hard ones, but there are other factors to consider—the shape and size of the seat and the angle of the back and material.

UPHOLSTERY OPTIONS If stains on upholstery are going to drive you crazy, get unupholstered chairs. Leather works well in the dining room because it's easy enough to clean and gets better with age. Patterned fabrics help hide spills, and outdoor or specially treated fabrics can make stains less of a big deal (downside: Stain-resistant chemicals are not so great for the environment).

buffet tables

PURPOSE These are multitasking pieces—a cache for linens and dishes, and a sideboard for dinner parties.

HEIGHT A buffet is typically taller than a dining table. Standard height is 36"; width and depth vary.

MATERIALS & STYLE Consider the buffet an opportunity to round out the room—it can visually balance the table and chairs, in form and finish.

OPEN OR CLOSED Most buffets are closed, but the open shelves in the picture above provide an airy counterpoint to a covered table and solid chairs. And think about whether you want your dishes and glasses on display. If you have pretty tableware, you might opt for open. In that case, neatness counts.

curtains

SOFTENING A ROOM Between all the "hard" furniture it contains—like table, chairs and buffet—and the legginess of the table, the dining room is a natural spot for fabrics. Even if you don't have them in other rooms, it might make sense to put up curtains here.

FABRICS & PATTERNS A foolproof way to pull together a room is to match curtains to the chair upholstery or, as in the room above, to a tablecloth. It's old-fashioned and straightforward, but it's cute and it works. In terms of volume, curtains should be full, not skimpy. A no-fail fabric formula for generous coverage is to order at least one and a half to two times the width of the window.

MOUNTS It is customary to hang a rod 4″ above the window frame and 6″ to 8″ past the frame on each side. Hanging higher can make the ceiling seem taller, while mounting wider can make your window appear bigger. Only mount curtains inside the frame if your window is very large.

lighting

CHANDELIER SIZE & HEIGHT Choosing a fixture one-third the length of the table is a good rule of thumb. The bottom of the fixture should hang 30″ to 34″ above the table. Have extra links on hand when hanging, and be there when the job is done: The only way to really tell if the height is right is to have someone stand on a ladder and hold the light above the table.

BULBS Round candelabra bulbs are good in modern fixtures. Use a simple torpedo-shaped bulb or a more ornate flame-shaped one in traditional chandeliers. To decide between frosted and clear varieties, buy and try both to see what looks better.

TABLE LAMPS & SCONCES Lighting at different levels—on the walls, on the buffet—makes the space warmer. Use dimmers everywhere for total mood mastery. And don't forget about the option of shutting off lights and using candles.

decorating tricks

FRAMING WALLPAPER makes it feel like a grand piece of art.

TRANSLUCENT CHAIRS keep a tight space from looking cluttered and lighten the mood of a heavy table.

ONE ODD STOOL tones down the formality of a coordinated dining set.

PALE BLUE ON THE CEILING adds soothing color to a neutral room.

SEATING A BIG CROWD can be affordable—forgo traditional dining chairs and invest in stackable stools.

more decorating tricks

A CUSTOM TABLE SKIRT transforms any old piece into an elegant buffet table and provides hidden storage.

ROSA ALBA *(Flore pleno)*   ROSIER BLANC ORDINAIRE

PAINTING THE CHAIRS of a traditional matching dining set updates the look.

CUSHIONS ARE AN EASY PLACE TO GO BOLD—try solids in different colors or a mix of related patterns, like these tartans.

A STENCILED FLOOR offers the pattern of a rug, but you can mop it clean.

AN OVERSCALE FIXTURE anchors an open dining space.

small-space solutions

A BANQUETTE TRANSFORMS a nook into a dining area and can offer built-in storage.

AGAINST A WINDOW, a table takes up about 3' less floor space (and can be pulled out for dinner parties).

A MIRRORED WALL gives the sensation of being in a much grander venue.

WITH A SCALED-DOWN TABLE, you can have all the elements of a proper dining room in tiny quarters.

EMBRACE THE SMALLNESS— lining an already tight room with bookcases enhances its coziness.

finishing touches

BETWEEN DINNER PARTIES, STYLE UP THE TABLE with stacks of books and objects.

MULTIPLE SHORT BOUQUETS are very conversation-friendly (no neck-craning necessary).

A GRAPHIC RUNNER is a lighter, more modern alternative to a full-on tablecloth.

LAYERED TABLECLOTHS, such as a patterned square over a plain solid, prove that two is more fun than one.

SUCCULENTS are an easy-care and long-lasting centerpiece.

the domino effect

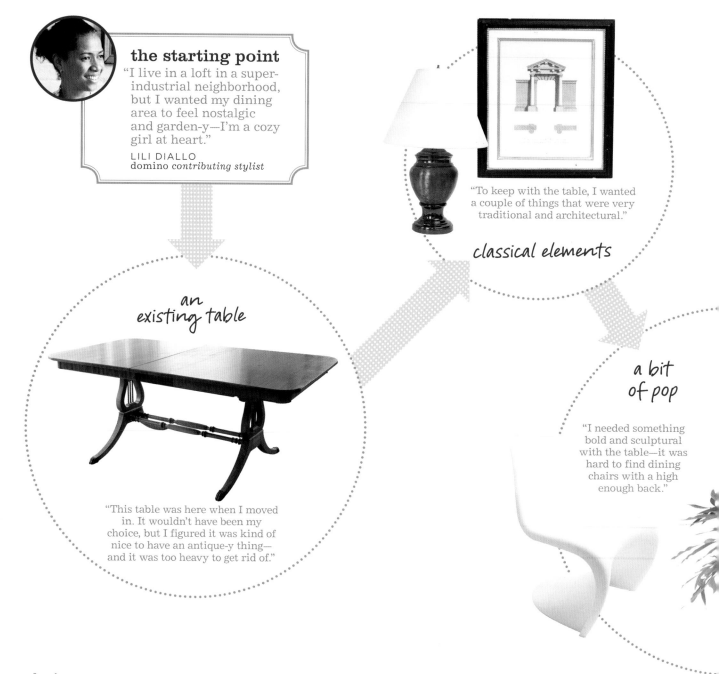

the starting point

"I live in a loft in a super-industrial neighborhood, but I wanted my dining area to feel nostalgic and garden-y—I'm a cozy girl at heart."

LILI DIALLO
domino *contributing stylist*

"To keep with the table, I wanted a couple of things that were very traditional and architectural."

classical elements

an existing table

"This table was here when I moved in. It wouldn't have been my choice, but I figured it was kind of nice to have an antique-y thing—and it was too heavy to get rid of."

a bit of pop

"I needed something bold and sculptural with the table—it was hard to find dining chairs with a high enough back."

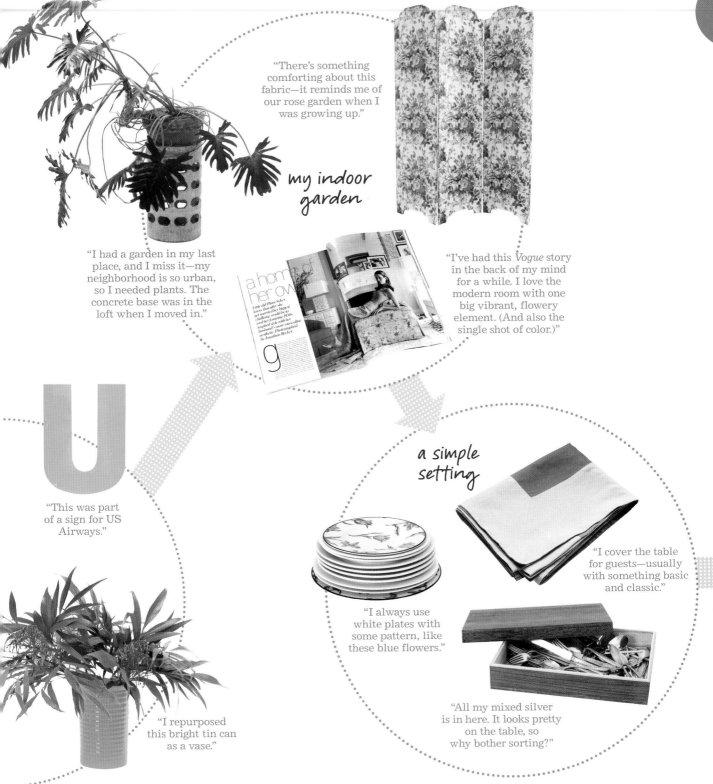

"There's something comforting about this fabric—it reminds me of our rose garden when I was growing up."

my indoor garden

"I had a garden in my last place, and I miss it—my neighborhood is so urban, so I needed plants. The concrete base was in the loft when I moved in."

"I've had this *Vogue* story in the back of my mind for a while. I love the modern room with one big vibrant, flowery element. (And also the single shot of color.)"

"This was part of a sign for US Airways."

a simple setting

"I cover the table for guests—usually with something basic and classic."

"I always use white plates with some pattern, like these blue flowers."

"I repurposed this bright tin can as a vase."

"All my mixed silver is in here. It looks pretty on the table, so why bother sorting?"

my dining room

"This is my little Proust 'madeleine moment.' The floral screen brings me back to my childhood. Some people have outdoor gardens—I have my chintz dining area." —LILI DIALLO

CHAPTER FIVE

the kitchen

the style:
vintage modern

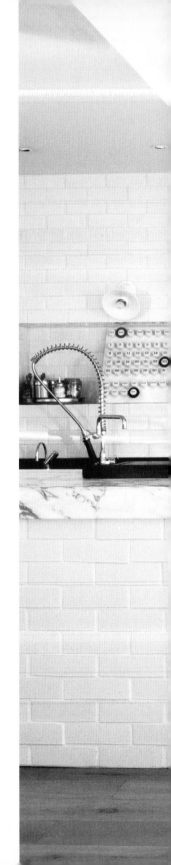

WHITE ON WHITE ON WHITE Subtle variations in hue and outspoken differences in styles and materials animate the one-color scheme. Shiny walls, two types of marble (one glossy and one matte, on the countertop and table, respectively), plus utilitarian ceramic sconces and an ornate porcelain chandelier provide a world of interest.

INDUSTRIAL COMPONENTS The kitchen is outfitted with restaurant-quality appliances, including a pot-scrubber faucet, an old-school scale and a massive stainless-steel stove and hood.

COLD AND WARM MATERIALS The time-worn look of Belgian baked-oak floorboards (waxed rather than stained for extra depth) and curvy, unfinished dining chairs balance the cool of the floor-to-ceiling tiles.

CONTEMPORARY LIFE Built-in nooks on either side of the stove accommodate a collection of cake stands, a pop '60s plastic calendar and a bright graphic letter. Personality permeates the space, and chairs clustered at the counter and a casual dining area make clear it is designed for family living.

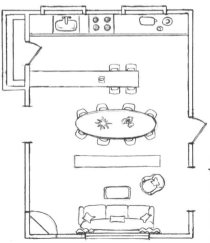

floor plan
The room has multiple zones, but all feel connected. The dining area is bordered by a long island and an open bookcase, which allows you to see through to a sitting nook.

Kitchen designed
by Ilse Crawford

the style:
refined
pastoral

OLD HOUSE, NEW SPACE The room lives in the present with stainless appliances, steel-legged tables and early-modern Thonet chairs but nods to the house's 19th-century past with countrified valances, subway tiling, historic paint colors and farmhouse-y storage baskets.

PRACTICAL SIMPLICITY Under- rather than overdecorated, the room is filled with casual, spontaneous solutions: A steel table stands in for cabinets, a metal bar–turned–pot rack hangs smack across a window and a plain narrow shelf sits atop the microwave. Weathered pans and a *tagine* are prominently on view, along with oils, spices and a crock of cooking utensils, all of which are easy to access.

BASIC, SOPHISTICATED HUES A subdued palette highlights the accessories on display, which are mostly black and white, keeping the scheme calm and soothing. The doors, trim and valances are also a quiet neutral, and the light-blue penny-tile floor is similarly unfussy.

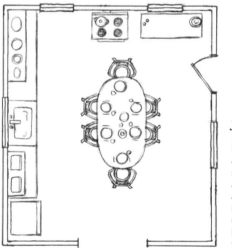

floor plan
Storage and prep areas are kept to a minimum, leaving ample space for a generously sized table ready to accommodate dinner parties, after-school snacking or homework projects. Having no upper cabinets makes this feel like more of a room than just a functional kitchen.

Kitchen of Sharon Simonaire,
interior designer

the style:
industrial glamour

SHINY SURFACES The mirrored backsplash and glossy white epoxy floor are essential elements in this polished, high-end mix. Gleaming stainless appliances and semiopaque glass cabinet faces also help amplify the available light.

LUXE CABINETRY Built with complicated profiles and finished with substantial, handsome hardware, the custom cabinets dress up the laboratory-like features.

MODERN ELEMENTS The stainless-steel table/island, professional stove, seamless floor and recessed counter lighting bring a muscular, utilitarian energy into an otherwise traditional space.

EFFICIENT & AIRY What feels like a large kitchen is actually quite compact. The built-in storage runs all the way to the ceiling and makes use of corners and wall space over doors, while the glass fronts and mirrors lighten the arrangement.

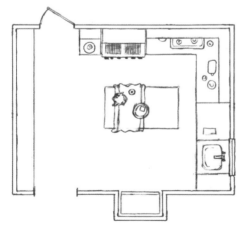

floor plan
Storage is maximized with a solid wall of floor-to-ceiling cabinets (far left) plus two short walls of upper and lower cabinets. The fridge tucks into a nook opposite the stove, freeing up space for the small prep table.

Kitchen designed
by Thomas O'Brien

the big piece: cabinets

UPPER CABINETS

Above-the-counter styles date to the early 20th century. Doors can be solid or have inset panels made of clear, frosted or wavy Restoration Glass (new glass fabricated to look old).

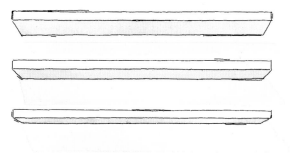

OPEN SHELVES

Light and airy—the lack of upper cabinets makes a kitchen feel more like a room. Great for displaying objects and keeping high-use pieces handy.

STAINLESS STEEL

Industrial appearance can be toned down by a warm countertop like wood. Shows fingerprints and can accumulate scratches over time; a powder-coated paint job can add color and keep fingerprints at bay.

WOOD

Organic and cozy. Best finishes:
a very pale, bleached effect or
a very dark, almost black stain.

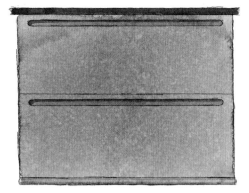

CUSTOMIZABLE MODERN SYSTEM

Sleek and built to function (think Boffi,
Poggenpohl, Alno). The ultimate in organization,
with the feel of a European race car.

LAMINATE

Neat-looking and subtle, which helps play
up hardware, counters and other elements.
Simple enough to look good in a color.

PANELED

Modern simplicity meets old-world
craftsmanship. Best when painted.

INSTANT EXPERT: buying cabinets

STANDARD SIZES
Base cabinets are usually
34½" tall and 24" deep.
The width increases in 3"
increments. Upper cabinets
range in height but are
generally 12" deep. Upper
cabinets are usually hung 16"
to 18" above countertops.

STOCK VS. CUSTOM
In terms of both styles and
sizes, off-the-shelf options
are limited, but prices are
lower and delivery times
shorter. Semicustom cabinets
offer additional styles, colors
and storage features but,
like stock, come only in
standard-size increments,
so you might end up
installing filler panels to close
gaps between the cabinet
and wall. Go custom and
you'll have total control over
aesthetics, functionality
and fit. You can play with
counter height, colors,
flourishes and profiles and
perfectly maximize your
kitchen's layout.

CABINETS VS. DRAWERS
Instead of lower cabinets,
many people prefer drawers,
which provide ready access
without digging.

how to mix & match

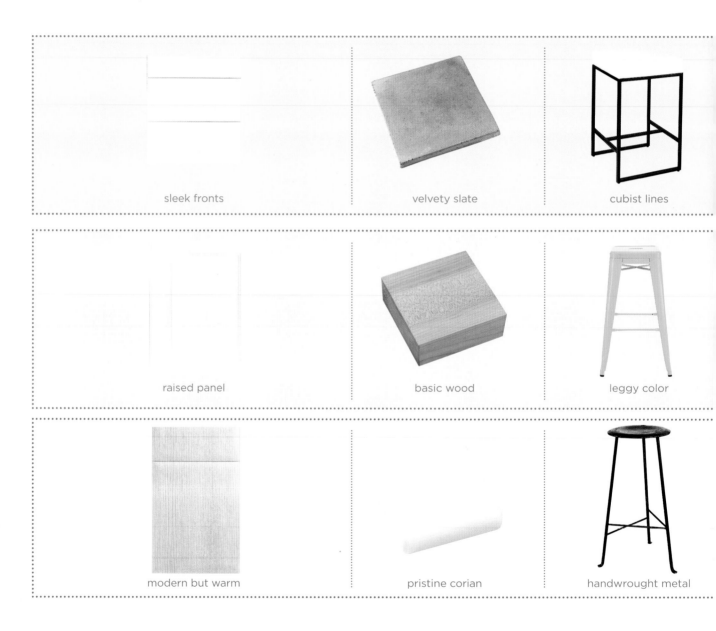

sleek fronts

velvety slate

cubist lines

raised panel

basic wood

leggy color

modern but warm

pristine corian

handwrought metal

utilitarian chic

streamlined stainless

Uniformly minimalist and functional, this setup makes a clear statement of **industrial Euro cool**. Everything is absolutely smooth to the touch, stripped-down and unapologetically high-design.

no-fuss shine

easy-bake cheer

You don't need the whole box of crayons to build a space that's **cute, bright and happy**. A canary-yellow stool and stove have all the electricity required to light up a neutral, can't-go-wrong assemblage of pendant lamps, wood countertops and classic cabinets.

playful baroque

haute-tech oven

Pickled-wood cabinets, spare white countertops and appliances, and a rough-hewn stool set the tone of this **sophisticated Swedish** look. A curvy white-resin chandelier is the un-kitchen-y wild card that keeps it from being too stark.

very important tips

counter/backsplash

WHERE TO START Cabinets set the kitchen's tone, but counters and backsplashes allow you to make the space your own. Be creative but also realistic: Pick a material that suits your life-style. You might love butcher block, but do you have time to keep up the necessary maintenance? Or love marble but will freak out over the inevitable marks?

CLASSIC COUNTER CHOICES The standard is a large slab counter and a backsplash of small tiles. Butcher block is inviting, stainless steel is sleek and marble can swing old-world or modern. Eco-friendly quartz composites, engineered to mimic natural stone, work in a variety of settings.

ONE MATERIAL OR TWO Juxtaposing two materials is more common, but using the same on both surfaces creates a seamless effect. Large, single slabs look cleaner than multiple tiles but are more expensive.

ALTERNATIVE BACKSPLASHES Because backsplashes aren't subject to the same use as countertops, you have some freedom with the materials. Think about installing a sheet of Plexiglas over a favorite wallpaper or using pressed-tin ceiling tiles or mirror.

sinks/faucets

MOUNTING Sinks may be dropped into a countertop (leaving the sink's rim visible) or undermounted (slipped below the counter). Generally, undermount sinks have a sharper look and are easier to keep clean than drop-ins.

STAINLESS VS. PORCELAIN SINK This depends on personal taste, maintenance compulsions (porcelain stains, stainless spots) and a kitchen's style. Stainless feels modern or industrial, while porcelain can read as elegant or country.

SELECTING A FAUCET A modern kitchen calls for a modern faucet (a traditional design would look out of place). In a traditional kitchen, however, you don't have to go fussy Victorian. A more streamlined tap can fit right in. Whatever you choose should be functional and comfortable to handle.

lighting/hardware

LIGHT PLACEMENT Think about how you use the room: You'll probably want more focused illumination for the spaces where you cook, more ambience for dining areas. It's common in kitchens to repeat a light, so go ahead and double or triple up if it suits your purpose.

UNCONVENTIONAL OPTIONS Lights normally found in living or dining rooms can add a lot of character: Consider a chandelier rather than a standard kitchen light. A small table lamp tucked in a corner instantly makes the space more homey.

SIMPLE HARDWARE Handsome pulls and hinges can make a moderately priced kitchen look a lot richer. Avoid gimmicks: Knobs shaped like corn on the cob might seem like a good idea, but these details should complement the kitchen as a whole, rather than call attention to themselves.

FUNCTION Before you buy a piece, hold it: The right hardware is as much about feel as it is about looks. Pulls versus knobs is a matter of personal preference, but for heavily used doors or drawers, pulls are usually the way to go.

floors

INDUSTRIAL Glossy epoxy yields an unbroken surface that can make small spaces seem bigger. Factory-chic concrete is great for those who want something edgier underfoot. Done in bright colors, rubber can be fun and highly functional: cushion-y for the cook, slip-free for the kids.

WARM If you want a softer look, or spend a lot of time on your feet cooking or washing up, think about wood, engineered wood or bamboo. For even more resiliency, try cork. Eco-friendly linoleum now comes in sophisticated colors and is as inexpensive as ever. Graphic patterns like a two-color stripe, a plaid or a dramatic field of all-black are very modern.

decorating tricks

> **A CONTINUOUS PATTERN**
> across counter and backsplash
> is graphic and unexpected.

ACRYLIC SHELVING preserves the purity of a colorful wall.

A BUILT-IN DESK in the kitchen is a small indulgence that makes a multitasker's life easier.

BRIGHT, WIDE STRIPES draw attention away from less-than-stellar cabinets and countertops.

APPLIANCES NEED NOT BE ALL STAINLESS—white or colored ones can add a bit of joy to a basic kitchen.

more decorating tricks

COLORFUL, MODERN CABINETS are a happy alternative to sleek white designer systems.

VINYL WALLPAPER as backsplash is glamorous, practical and economical too.

A WHOLE WALL OF TILE reads like wallpaper (but it's simpler to clean).

LIVING-ROOM FURNITURE IN THE KITCHEN makes a utilitarian space feel decorated.

HORIZONTAL STRIPES fool the eye—a narrow galley kitchen suddenly looks wider.

small-space solutions

DITCHING THE UPPERS in favor of open shelving lightens the look but still holds everything that a cabinet can.

A WALL-MOUNTED ORGANIZER lets a petite kitchen multitask as office.

MINI APPLIANCES, including a two-burner stove, and a tiny sink make it possible to squeeze a "full" kitchen into a compact corner.

CARVE A BREAKFAST NOOK out of the tightest space using a scaled-down table and stools that tuck underneath.

A READY-MADE, ALL-IN-ONE UNIT—with stovetop, fridge, sink and storage—is ideal for cramped apartments.

tricks for renters

DARK WALLS and a door painted a contrasting color quickly transform even the humblest rental.

SET UP A FULL-TIME BAR in the kitchen if your life-style is more about cocktail hour than dinner parties.

A PLATE RACK is extra kitchen storage you can take with you when you move.

A PRETTY LACE VALANCE gussies up a style-challenged rental kitchen.

TURN A PLAIN-JANE FRIDGE into a garden of flowers with wallpaper (maybe check with your landlord first).

the domino effect

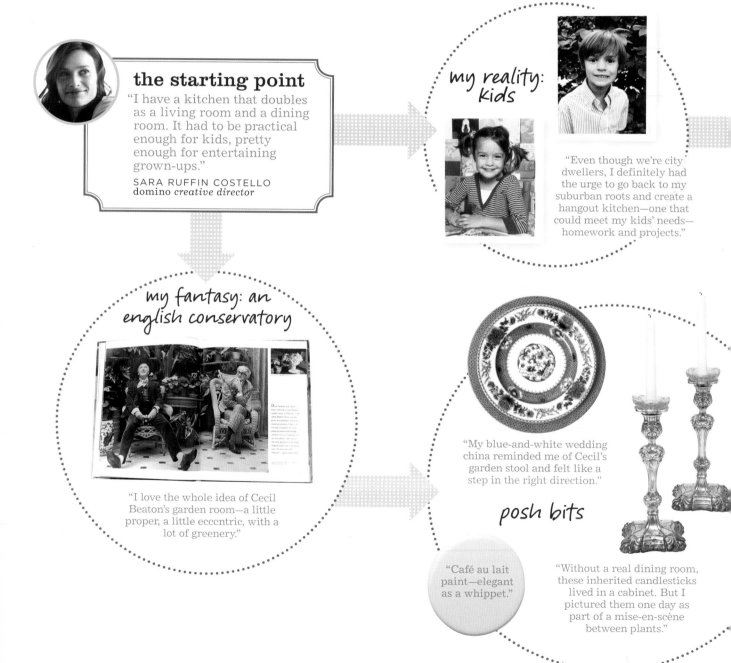

the starting point

"I have a kitchen that doubles as a living room and a dining room. It had to be practical enough for kids, pretty enough for entertaining grown-ups."

SARA RUFFIN COSTELLO
domino *creative director*

my reality: kids

"Even though we're city dwellers, I definitely had the urge to go back to my suburban roots and create a hangout kitchen—one that could meet my kids' needs—homework and projects."

my fantasy: an english conservatory

"I love the whole idea of Cecil Beaton's garden room—a little proper, a little eccentric, with a lot of greenery."

"My blue-and-white wedding china reminded me of Cecil's garden stool and felt like a step in the right direction."

posh bits

"Café au lait paint—elegant as a whippet."

"Without a real dining room, these inherited candlesticks lived in a cabinet. But I pictured them one day as part of a mise-en-scène between plants."

"Since the island is the center of the room, the faucet there needed to be more than just functional. This one has height and elegance."

practical considerations

"Giant drawers with equally substantial hardware give this kitchen lots of storage plus a little drama."

"Upholstery's almost never used on kitchen stools for a good reason. So I was happy to find this Moroccan oilcloth—chic and spillproof."

"I've had this classic table in every one of my apartments. It's small enough to fit in the kitchen, but you can squeeze in six people."

simple shapes

"I wanted houseplants that have great forms, and an oversize topiary was the obvious place to begin."

"This burlap-covered Louis settee was a major score—perfectly diminutive and actually comfortable."

my kitchen

"It's actually a high-functioning studio apartment—everything from taxes to massively messy art projects to dinner parties happens here."

—SARA RUFFIN COSTELLO

CHAPTER SIX

the bedroom

the style:
romantic modernist

SPARKLY NEUTRAL PALETTE Soft "greige" walls, a milky canopy and shiny metallic accessories create a peaceful space that's cool and refined. Silver and cream go together like pieces in a formal place setting.

PAINT BED CURTAINS SHEETS BLANKET

SLEEK COCOON The long drapes, which break gently on the floor and stretch all the way to the ceiling, feel structural and columnlike. The bed is warm and inviting, yet sparely made with Euro shams, standard pillows and a tucked-in quilt—nothing frilly.

SIMPLE SHAPES, SUPPLE TEXTURES The bedside tables, lamps and frames share a clean-lined aesthetic that's tempered by sensuous materials (wood, glass, silver). The same idea is at play on the bed, where sateen sheets balance out the heavy-duty linen bed skirt and drapes. A small chintz pillow offers the room's single moment of pattern.

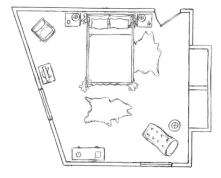

floor plan
The queen bed flanked by bedside tables is oriented to have prime views of the windows. A nearby chair makes the most of a tight angle. In the opposite corner, a chaise and a floor lamp form a reading nook.

Bedroom of Dara
Caponigro, domino
style director

the style:
sweet
asceticism

SIMPLEST PINK, OTHERWISE WHITE This super-minimal scheme plays the sugariness of pale pink off the coolness of white to create an oasis of calm. The white also functions as a border, emphasizing the geometry of the space.

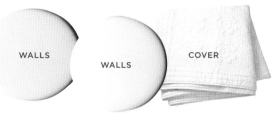

WALLS WALLS COVER

SPARENESS BEGETS SERENITY The furnishings are spartan and the walls bare, which encourages an instant melting away of mental clutter. Unembellished bed linens, angular table lamps and white wood blinds are clean and streamlined, and the glossy painted floors reflect light.

FLOATING FURNITURE With a raised platform bed and leggy side tables, everything is off the ground and airy-feeling.

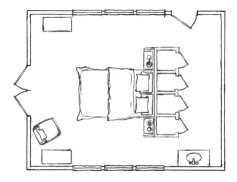

floor plan
The bed tucks into a freestanding alcove wall, which serves as a headboard and separates the sleeping area from the bathroom—a sink plus four closets (that house a toilet, a shower, clothes and linens).

Bedroom of Camilla and
Benjamin Trigano, *marketing
director and gallery owner*

the style:
sophisticated froufrou

RICH FABRICS With its cranberry-red flowers and black branches, the curtain print is a spunky take on regal chinoiserie. Pea-soup-green velvet makes the formal, tufted headboard feel even more luxurious.

CURTAINS HEADBOARD BEDDING

BLACK TONES DOWN THE GIRLINESS A dark ceiling delivers high drama and guarantees that even with all the ruffles and flowers, the room isn't stereotypically feminine.

SERIOUS WITH FLIRTY DETAILS The classic, tidy bedmaking is tempered by an unexpected mix of styles—tailored hotel borders with scalloped matelassé. Abundant wraparound curtains and a valance are fairly proper, but funny flea-market lamps and mismatched bedside tables lighten the mood and keep the look young.

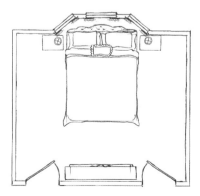

floor plan
Bay windows can be a challenge, but here they're used to great advantage as a framing device, cradling the bed. A large armoire, fit snugly between the doors, offers ample storage.

Bedroom of Chloe Warner,
interior decorator

the style:
masculine bohemian

STRONG COLORS AND PATTERNS Confident dark stripes appear in varied scales—from the broad-banded area rug to the narrow-striped duvet—and ground the room's theatricality with a bit of New England prep. Rich-brown walls provide a warm, enveloping backdrop.

RUG CHAIRS CHAIR WALLS

NEW MIXED WITH OLD A mélange of antique pieces—a grisaille screen, unique bedside tables and lamps, and a knobby chair—soften a very modern steel bed. Coordinated lamp shades and simple curtains keep a lid on the eccentricity.

UNUSUAL ACCESSORIES There aren't a lot of accent pieces here, but all of them are out of the ordinary, including the ornate and shell-encrusted lamps, the screen and the uplit figure of St. John the Baptist.

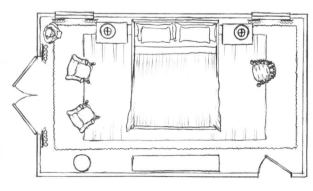

floor plan
This bedroom is an inviting hangout spot, thanks to three occasional chairs oriented around the bed as if it were a sofa. Layered rugs enhance the cocoon-y feel of the large four-poster bed.

Bedroom of Johnson Hartig,
fashion designer

the big piece: beds

MODERN PLATFORM
Low, minimalist, masculine. Substantial but works well in small spaces because it has no footboard.

IRON CANOPY
Style dates back to 18th-century France. Feminine, grand. Floats nicely in the middle of a room. With a canopy of fabric, it's even more romantic; bare, it's architectural.

FOUR-POSTER
This form dates to the 15th century, but there are very modern options. Tall and commanding, it can make ceilings seem higher.

UPHOLSTERED

Glamorous and luxurious, yet handsome. The padded back is comfortable for reading in bed. Nail-head trim and piping can be used to accentuate the shape.

BAROQUE

Style dates back to 17th-century Europe. Intricately carved wood headboard. Opulent and majestic. Consider keeping other furnishings spare and modern.

SLEIGH

Wood versions hail back to the Roman Empire. Contemporary upholstered ones are more comfortable.

COUNTRY SWEDISH

Delicate but unpretentious. Straight or curved high head- and footboards, with panels sometimes upholstered or caned.

INSTANT EXPERT: buying a mattress

STUFFING Traditional innerspring mattresses are made of steel coils topped by padding (usually foam, felt and polyester or cotton fibers) and wrapped in a fabric cover. Eco-friendly options include those made of untreated, organic cotton; chemical-free wool; or natural latex (as opposed to the synthetic variety).

COMFORT TESTING Spend plenty of time reclining on the models you like. That blissful first impression can be deceiving. Pillow tops, aka the final layer of padding, come in many thicknesses, and stores' floor models tend to sport the thickest version. If you prefer something firmer, ask to test other options.

CHECK THE COIL COUNT This refers to the number of springs inside—the higher, the better. But a coil count tops out at about 400 for a queen—beyond that, you'll unlikely feel a difference. **BTW:** This is a moot point for latex mattresses, which are coil-free.

BOX SPRING You may not need one. A bed frame that has a base to support a mattress (slats, for instance) can usually do without. But if you like to climb into bed, literally, a box spring can give you that extra height.

how to mix & match

tufted elegance

carved stand

crisp bedding

tropical four-poster

featherweight polish

cheery coverlet

solid foundation

boxy accents

ethnic texture

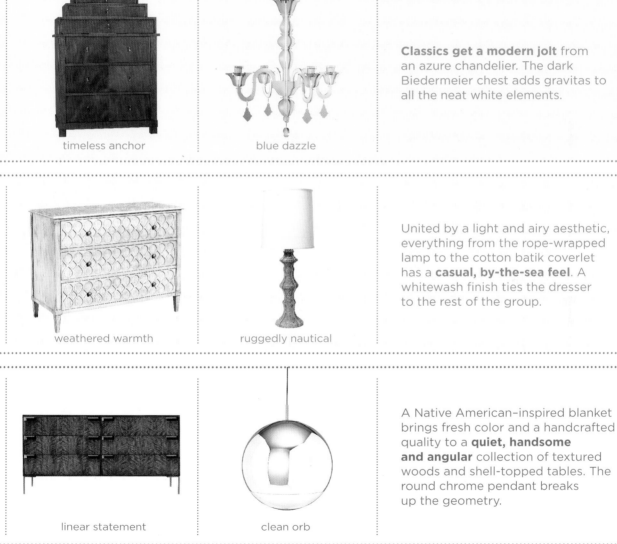

why these pieces work together

timeless anchor

blue dazzle

Classics get a modern jolt from an azure chandelier. The dark Biedermeier chest adds gravitas to all the neat white elements.

weathered warmth

ruggedly nautical

United by a light and airy aesthetic, everything from the rope-wrapped lamp to the cotton batik coverlet has a **casual, by-the-sea feel**. A whitewash finish ties the dresser to the rest of the group.

linear statement

clean orb

A Native American–inspired blanket brings fresh color and a handcrafted quality to a **quiet, handsome and angular** collection of textured woods and shell-topped tables. The round chrome pendant breaks up the geometry.

very important tips

bedside tables

DIMENSIONS As a general rule, the table should be about the same height as the mattress. Deep tables (anything beyond 24") make it difficult to get in and out of bed.

COMPOSITION The simplest thing is to top matching tables with matching lamps. But tables and lamps certainly don't have to be in matching pairs. If you vary one of the tables, for instance, use two of the same lamp or vice versa.

STORAGE Most people like to have drawers or shelves, but minimalist types can use any beautiful table. If you fall in love with a table that doesn't have a drawer, tuck a smaller table or stool underneath as a place to stow books or a phone.

LIGHTING Install a dimmer switch if you can. If your lamp has two bulbs and no dimmer switch, using two different-wattage bulbs lets you control the mood: 40 watts for ambience and 60 to 75 watts for reading. Non-opaque shades are ideal for reading. If space is at a premium, consider installing sconces.

window treatments

INFORMAL VS. FORMAL Generally speaking, shades are casual and curtains formal, but both options can swing either way: You can dress up a shade by using a more formal fabric (above) or dress down a drape with a casual one. Because they require less fabric, shades are usually cheaper.

PATTERN AND COLOR Bedrooms tend to be more matchy and romantic than other rooms, so you can go as far as you want in coordinating your window treatments with other components in the room. Coordinate them with your wallpaper, chairs and/or bed skirt—the more pieces you include, the more "done" the room will appear. As an alternative, you can simply pick up on the room's colors, as in the photo above.

BLACKOUT Both shades and curtains can be lined with blackout fabric to block light. Hang blackout shades behind curtains for maximum darkness.

MOUNTS For shades, inside mounts (above) fit inside the window frame; outside mounts run from outside edge to outside edge of the frame (see photos to the left and right) and can make the window look bigger. Curtains, however, are almost always mounted outside the window frame.

rugs

AREA RUGS A large rug can unify a room, but in order to maximize its impact, it needs to be big enough not to disappear when topped by a bed. In an ideal world, the bed is either entirely off or on the rug, but as long as about three-quarters of the rug is under the bed, it's okay.

THROW RUGS Helpful in dividing the room into zones, a small rug and a bench at the foot of the bed can demarcate a seating area. Placed on each side of the bed, a throw rug in a soft material makes a luxurious landing pad (above). To add more texture, layer smaller rugs over larger area rugs.

WALL-TO-WALL Because it's the place you're most likely to be barefoot and least likely to spill food, the bedroom is ideal for allover carpeting. Natural fibers like wool are always a good bet.

bedding

SHEETS Natural materials like cotton and linen feel best and, if of high quality, age beautifully. How to choose? Feel before you buy. Thread counts are not the be-all and end-all. Some manufacturers count the thin strands that make up a thread, which can triple or even quadruple the final score.

MIXING AND MATCHING SHEETS The easiest way to combine different patterns is to make sure they share the same background color (such as white or ivory).

BEYOND STANDARD PILLOWS Built for looks rather than sleeping, square Euro shams (24") are also fine props for reading; a petite boudoir pillow is a sweet finishing touch. If you have a king-size bed, be sure to use king-size pillows to fill the bed's whole width.

BED SKIRTS Ready-mades usually come in three styles: kick pleat, box pleat and ruffle. When buying, make sure to get the correct length by measuring from the top of the box spring to the floor—a too-long skirt looks sloppy and too short looks silly. A custom version can pull together a room when the bed skirt is done in a fabric used elsewhere in the room. Lining makes it look more substantial, and prewashing the fabric before it's sewn prevents future shrinkage.

decorating tricks

UPHOLSTERED WALLS imbue a bedroom with warmth and coziness.

A DIY CANOPY is a low-cost and easy alternative to a proper four-poster.

ONE COLORFUL CHANDELIER can carry a neutral room.

A DESK CAN DOUBLE AS A BEDSIDE TABLE—it's often the same height as the average bed.

A SOLID CANVAS ABOVE THE BED is a graphic substitute for a headboard.

more decorating tricks

GRIDDED FAMILY PHOTOS make a striking installation. The frames are duct-taped together at the back and hung as a unit.

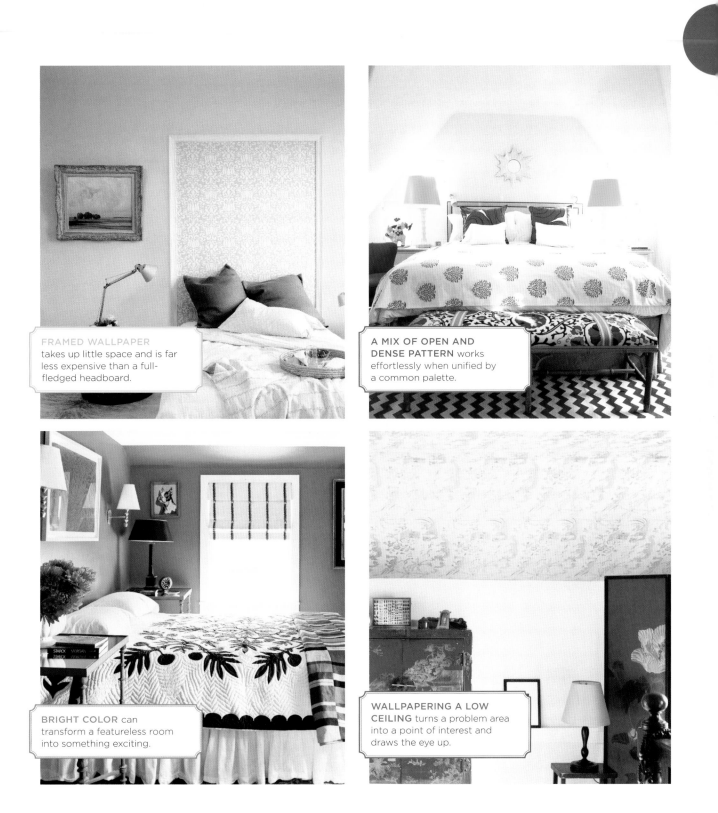

FRAMED WALLPAPER takes up little space and is far less expensive than a full-fledged headboard.

A MIX OF OPEN AND DENSE PATTERN works effortlessly when unified by a common palette.

BRIGHT COLOR can transform a featureless room into something exciting.

WALLPAPERING A LOW CEILING turns a problem area into a point of interest and draws the eye up.

small-space solutions

CREATE TWO ZONES in one room, with a love seat as the bridge.

BOLD CURTAINS are a space-saving alternative to bi-fold closet doors.

FLOAT A SHELF above the bed if there's no room for a proper bedside table.

A SHADE AND CURTAINS CONCEAL STORAGE and form a sweet nook for sleeping.

EXUBERANT COLORS in high-gloss convert a big closet into a bedroom.

making the bed

A BEAUTIFUL TEXTILE AS COVERLET is charming and bohemian—just pull it up to the headboard and add a few pillows in different patterns that share a hue (here, red).

COORDINATING THE COVERLET AND SHAMS is a no-fuss formula. A vivid blanket and throw pillow keep it from being boring.

THIS SUPER-FANCY ARRANGEMENT featuring eight flanged pillows and matching sheets requires a hot iron and a lot of starch. To balance the pillow madness: a matching duvet neatly folded at the foot.

FOR THIS NO-MAINTENANCE MOD setup, fluff the duvet (you don't even need a top sheet—that's how the Europeans do it), crown with two bright throw pillows and go.

THE RECIPE FOR A WELL-MADE (AND REALISTIC) BED: sheets, pillowcases, tucked-in coverlet, folded blanket and one throw pillow. Nothing more, nothing less.

the domino effect

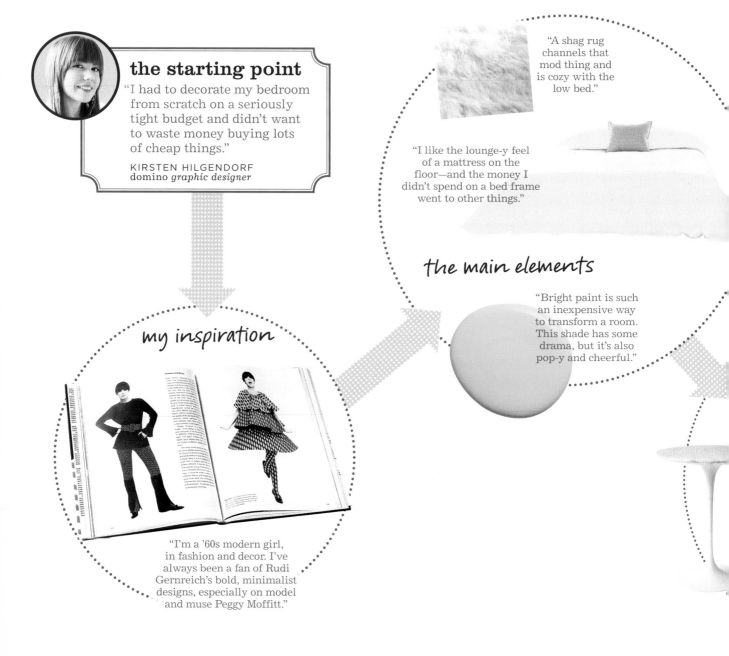

the starting point

"I had to decorate my bedroom from scratch on a seriously tight budget and didn't want to waste money buying lots of cheap things."

KIRSTEN HILGENDORF
domino *graphic designer*

my inspiration

"I'm a '60s modern girl, in fashion and decor. I've always been a fan of Rudi Gernreich's bold, minimalist designs, especially on model and muse Peggy Moffitt."

"A shag rug channels that mod thing and is cozy with the low bed."

"I like the lounge-y feel of a mattress on the floor—and the money I didn't spend on a bed frame went to other things."

the main elements

"Bright paint is such an inexpensive way to transform a room. This shade has some drama, but it's also pop-y and cheerful."

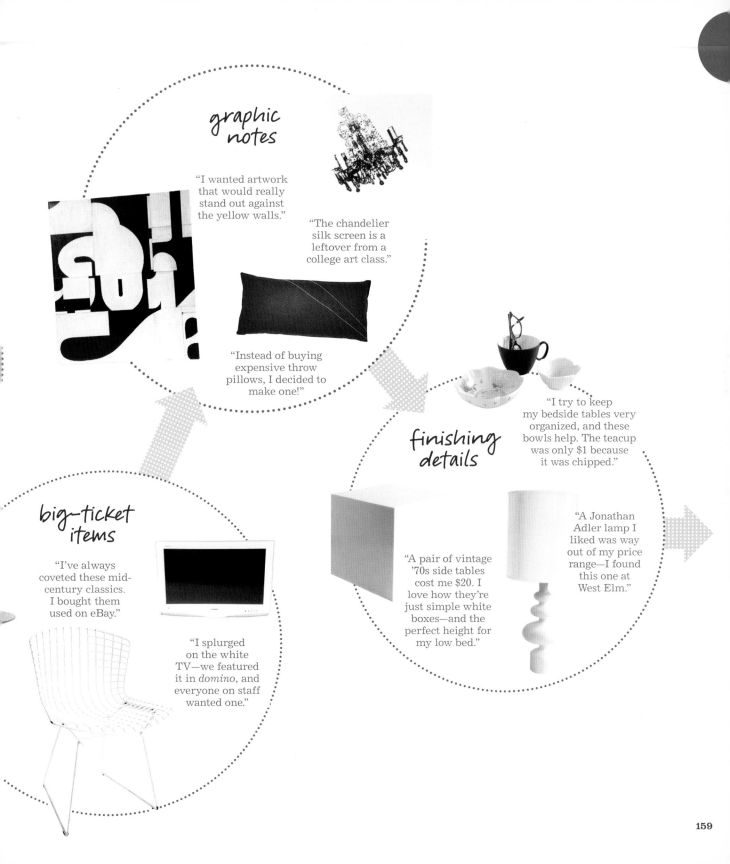

graphic notes

"I wanted artwork that would really stand out against the yellow walls."

"The chandelier silk screen is a leftover from a college art class."

"Instead of buying expensive throw pillows, I decided to make one!"

finishing details

"I try to keep my bedside tables very organized, and these bowls help. The teacup was only $1 because it was chipped."

"A Jonathan Adler lamp I liked was way out of my price range—I found this one at West Elm."

"A pair of vintage '70s side tables cost me $20. I love how they're just simple white boxes—and the perfect height for my low bed."

big-ticket items

"I've always coveted these mid-century classics. I bought them used on eBay."

"I splurged on the white TV—we featured it in *domino*, and everyone on staff wanted one."

my bedroom

"This room is totally easygoing. It's about kicking back, listening to records and waking up to sunshine (even on a cloudy day)."

—KIRSTEN HILGENDORF

CHAPTER SEVEN

the bathroom

the style:
rustic zen

MOODY PALETTE Deep, sumptuous blacks (on the walls, window shade and tub exterior) give this bathroom its edge. In contrast, the porcelain tub interior has an almost celestial brilliance.

WARM TEXTURES Brass fittings, an earthy plaster wall and an amber glass pendant add depth and sheen to the somber elements. The herringbone wood floor has a worn, imperfect quality that imbues the space with a certain European character.

SCULPTURAL ELEMENTS The components are minimal— only a claw-foot tub, an exposed shower pipe, a pendant and a towel rack—but set in isolation, each feels architectural and luxurious.

OPEN LAYOUT The bathroom flows into the bedroom, evoking a seductive antechamber. A rich oriental rug hovering at the threshold adds to the roomlike atmosphere. With the toilet separate and hidden behind doors, this is a true retreat.

Bathroom of Jenna Lyons
Mazeau and Vincent Mazeau,
creative director and artist

the style:
girly drama

CONFECTIONERY FLOURISHES This scheme defies
the unremarkable bones of the space by establishing a visual identity
with color and pattern. The pink is unabashedly feminine, but using
it in two very different scales—wide painted stripes and a small zigzag
shower curtain—lends it sophistication.

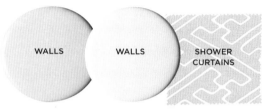

WALLS   WALLS   SHOWER
                              CURTAINS

A BIT OF THEATER Bold stripes converge on the ceiling,
forming a trompe l'oeil circus tent. The shower curtains, treated like
fancy drapes (complete with tiebacks), heighten the ta-da effect; the
tub becomes a stage. A vintage chandelier introduces a curlicue shape
to counter all the strong lines.

DRESSY DETAILS Clever little touches—from whimsical
drawer pulls that revitalize basic white cabinets to a pretty blue tray
for perfumes—complete the transformation from blah and boring
to glamorous.

Bathroom of Krista Ewart,
interior decorator

the style:
hotel luxe

CLEAN, OPULENT SURFACES Marble, marble everywhere—on the floor, surrounding the tub, even traveling up the wall—conjures a posh English estate. Mirrors inset into the molding create the illusion of an even grander space. Classic fittings like the nickel-and-porcelain, telephone-style bath fixture enhance the old-world feel.

REAL FURNITURE An antique bureau, a stately lamp and a suede-and-brass stool (no white laminate here) are lavish yet bring warmth and character to the room.

SPA HERE, STUFF THERE One side of the room remains hotel-like and pristine, with the marble-framed tub, simple white towels and uncluttered planes. Personal tchotchkes and toiletries stay on the bureau side.

Bathroom of Allison Sarofim,
domino contributing editor

the big piece: sinks

WASHSTAND

*Old-world styling is graceful
and light. A large flat top
(typically marble) holds
essentials, and a crossbar hangs
towels. Visible plumbing. Legs
come in glass, acrylic or metal.*

PEDESTAL

*Comes in traditional, modern and
Art Deco versions. Simple base
hides plumbing and takes up little
floor space. Top can be flat, which
will hold a few items.*

BOWL ON TOP

*Sculptural, decorative
and dramatic. More
about style than function.
Perfect for a statement-
making powder room.*

WALL MOUNT

*This legless option keeps the floor clear.
Available in various styles and shapes, including
corner options great for tiny spaces.*

OPEN VANITY

*Has a lighter appearance than a
closed unit. A single shelf offers a
place to stack towels or hold
a basket. The large basin is part
of the piece's architecture.*

VANITY

*Ample storage below and on top. Works
well in two-sink versions.
With legs, feels more like a piece of furniture.*

CONSOLE

*Made entirely of porcelain,
from legs to backsplash, this
romantic piece feels right for an
old house. A nice option in the
double-sink version.*

INSTANT EXPERT: buying a faucet

STICK WITH ONE LOOK
Pick a faucet that's in keeping with the style of your sink. This is not a place to experiment (e.g., putting a modern tap on a vintage-style sink).

MATERIALS
Good for modern baths, chrome is the cheapest option; nickel is warmer and pricier and works in modern or traditional settings. Unlacquered brass, especially "dirty brass," has an appealing patina.

FINISHES
You can't go wrong with bright and sparkly polished hardware on a modern sink. A brushed finish hides water stains but is more expensive.

ONE PIECE OR THREE
A "single-hole" faucet is all one piece—with handles and spout connected. "Center-set" faucets unite handles and spout on a 4" base. A "widespread" is three components—spout plus two handles. Check your sink's spread (the distance from center to center of the outer holes) before you buy.

how to mix & match

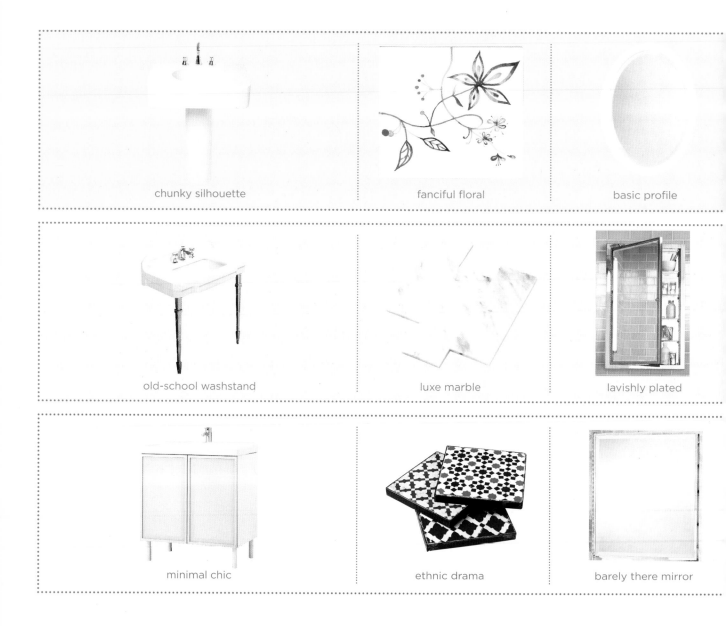

chunky silhouette

fanciful floral

basic profile

old-school washstand

luxe marble

lavishly plated

minimal chic

ethnic drama

barely there mirror

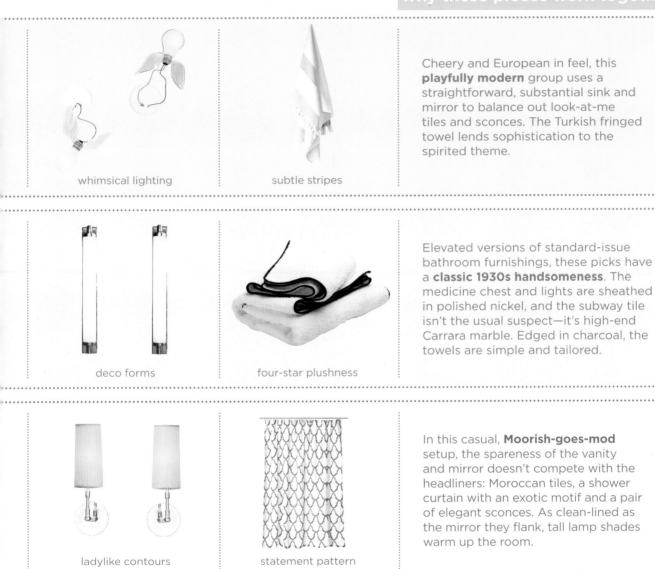

whimsical lighting

subtle stripes

Cheery and European in feel, this **playfully modern** group uses a straightforward, substantial sink and mirror to balance out look-at-me tiles and sconces. The Turkish fringed towel lends sophistication to the spirited theme.

deco forms

four-star plushness

Elevated versions of standard-issue bathroom furnishings, these picks have a **classic 1930s handsomeness**. The medicine chest and lights are sheathed in polished nickel, and the subway tile isn't the usual suspect—it's high-end Carrara marble. Edged in charcoal, the towels are simple and tailored.

ladylike contours

statement pattern

In this casual, **Moorish-goes-mod** setup, the spareness of the vanity and mirror doesn't compete with the headliners: Moroccan tiles, a shower curtain with an exotic motif and a pair of elegant sconces. As clean-lined as the mirror they flank, tall lamp shades warm up the room.

very important tips

fixtures & fittings

CHOOSING TUBS Depending on how much space you have, the layout of your bathroom and your style preferences, you can get a drop-in model (usually sunk into a platform), a corner unit that attaches to the wall or a freestanding one (these come in an array of styles besides claw foot, including many very modern ones, like the one above). Regardless of the model's shape or style, look for a tub that goes with your sink and toilet. A practical note: Freestanding tubs are romantic, but this old-fashioned design has old-fashioned limitations—namely, no supereasy way to include a shower (think wraparound curtain sticking to your legs).

TOILETS This is a good place to go the classic route. Toilets should also coordinate with your tub and sink. Seek out low-flow options that conserve water.

TOWEL BARS AND SHOWER RODS Typically bought as a suite, these fittings function best as a cohesive unit. Don't forget about hooks, which are useful, friendly and great for any and all towels.

lighting & mirrors

LIGHTING A combination of sources affords the most flexibility. Using a chandelier or sconces typically found in a dining room, or a table lamp that could be at home in a living room, is a great way to bring style to the bathroom and connect it to the rest of the house. Try a dimmer switch to tone down the glare during evening soaks in the tub.

SCONCES Sconces placed on either side of the mirror tend to cast flattering light, but one sconce over the mirror provides more focused illumination. To be safe, match finishes to the rest of your bathroom hardware.

MIRRORS AND MEDICINE CHESTS In a small bathroom, medicine chests are often a storage necessity. There are recessed and nonrecessed versions; the former is usually preferable because it's less intrusive, but it's more complicated to install. If you don't need the storage, a framed mirror adds a nice decorating note and feels less utilitarian than a medicine chest; in a powder room, a mirror is the natural choice.

floors & walls

MIXING MATERIALS Using one material from floor to ceiling (as above) creates a continuous, sleek skin that's more modern. Having two materials draws attention to the room's planes. Note that if you combine different types of tile, it's best to vary the scale.

FLOORING OPTIONS Matte tiles are less slippery than shiny ones. A wood floor is common in old houses and can look very handsome but does best when sealed. Marble can be luxurious—the bigger the slab, the fancier the effect and the more expensive. Bamboo is au courant and eco-friendly.

WALLPAPER This is an excellent way to usher in personality and color. It does well in powder rooms or guest bathrooms, where it won't be subject to a lot of moisture.

accessories

SHOWER CURTAINS The bathroom's major style statement can, of course, be bought ready-made, but if you don't find one to your liking or your tub doesn't accommodate a standard length (72" x 72"), go custom. Select an outdoor fabric and you can forgo a liner. Rings shouldn't be an afterthought—the right set is a nice finishing touch.

FURNITURE Whether you use it to hold a stack of towels, help you through your beauty routine or provide seating for someone to chat with during a bath, a small chair or stool is inviting (especially with terry-cloth upholstery).

decorating tricks

AN ORNATE MIRROR injects personality into a super-modern interior.

A PAINTED FAUX TENT turns a boxy bathroom into a graphic alternate reality.

SHIMMERING ELEMENTS like pearlescent tile reflect so much sun, you can leave off the lights.

LIVING-ROOM-STYLE CURTAINS in the shower are an elegant surprise. A curtain track (instead of a rod) heightens the effect.

A HAND-PAINTED MOTIF can have the drama of patterned wallpaper (without the risk of mold and peeling).

more decorating tricks

OUTFIT YOUR BATH WITH REAL FURNITURE (if you have the space)—think beyond terry cloth and chrome legs.

LINING A WHOLE ROOM WITH SMALL TILES makes surfaces seem almost reptilian.

A FREESTANDING TUB gives even the most modern bathroom a romantic edge.

A GLASS WALL, instead of a shower curtain, allows the room to feel as airy as possible.

WILD WALLPAPER in a powder room is a trippy surprise.

finishing touches

SIDE TABLES—like these water-resistant cork ones—can be both functional and beautiful under a sink or beside a tub.

CASUAL SNAPSHOTS AND POSTCARDS make a fun substitute for wallpaper.

MATCHING BASKETS that fit your shelves perfectly keep things artfully tidy.

A POTTED FERN thrives in the bathroom (it loves moisture!) and softens a stark space.

DRESS UP YOUR BATHROOM with the good stuff, like a collection of blue-and-white porcelain.

the domino effect

the starting point

"My house came with a small, ugly bathroom that was crying out for a gut renovation. I wanted to keep it low-cost and DIY."

CHASE BOOTH
domino *set producer*

"Finding this was a wonderful surprise. It let the outside in, and I just followed that lead, going organic and green wherever possible."

bringing in nature

"Like the ground outside, only richer."

"The fern is so happy in here because of the steam."

before the renovation

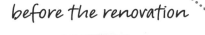

"This bathroom was a disaster, so I began by tearing everything out. I was a novice but knew I wanted simple materials—nothing ostentatious. When I tore down the vinyl-covered walls, I uncovered my real decorating inspiration—a huge hidden double window."

rustic notes

"I saw this in a Green Issue of *domino*. It reminds me of this magnificent shag-bark hickory tree on my property."

"A hand-carved teak stool where I put my glass of wine, my candle and my book—comfort central."

classic elements

"The sink was rescued from a Fifth Avenue renovation—it would have been trashed."

"Subway and penny tile—clean, neutral and timeless."

finishing touches

"I'm not a big fan of curtain rods. With a track on the ceiling, the hardware just disappears. I made a linen curtain that goes all the way to the floor, and the result is really dramatic."

"A beautiful contrast with the brown on the walls—fresh and kind of delightful."

"An Edison bulb on this industrial fixture throws off the most flattering, warm yellow light."

my bathroom

"It's like being in a serene grotto, with the earthy walls, the gentle breeze and the fern overhead."

—CHASE BOOTH

CHAPTER EIGHT

the office

the style:
rich & handsome

WARM TEXTURES All of the surfaces are covered, from the sea-grass walls to the dark trellis-chain-link rug, providing a luxurious, tactile enclosure for layers of books, furnishings and objets.

WALLS   RUG   SHADES   CHAIR   CHAIR

UNIFIED PALETTE A disciplined color scheme dominated by browns can support a few contrasting patterns without looking off-kilter. The prints on the rug, chair and window shades offer graphic drama that accentuates the sumptuous beauty.

STORAGE AS DISPLAY Reproductions of Anglo-Indian bookshelves hold a well-considered collection of books and small-scale art. The careful placement of stacks alongside portraits and ephemera creates an intriguing yet ordered tableau.

UNCONVENTIONAL FURNITURE A shapely chair upholstered in suede and another wearing a tiger print provide major impact not usually seen in an office.

floor plan
Formerly a spare bedroom, this large study has an open, hospitable feeling, thanks to a living-room-like seating area. Freestanding bookcases on both ends of the room are a low-commitment alternative to built-ins in this rental apartment.

Office of Markham Roberts,
interior decorator

the style:
functional chic

RECASTING A PLAIN SPACE This room started life as a garage (a shed or attic would fit the bill too) and was reinvented with a wash of white, on everything from the floors to the shelves. Floor-to-ceiling doors let in plenty of light and foster an indoor-outdoor ease.

OPEN ORGANIZATION Though the all-white scheme communicates a crisp vision, the room also has a no-nonsense utility. The glossy file cabinet is in full view, and one wall is completely given over to shelving. Inexpensive uniform storage boxes impart a tidy look to the shelves, despite being chockful of supplies.

CHROMATIC UNITY The envelope of bright white creates a fresh, motivating background, underscored by the super-polished and painted cement floor. Pops of red—in storage boxes and throw pillows—bring contrast into the one-color space.

SOFT TOUCHES A large, slightly wild plant in one corner adds a natural element to a room that could otherwise feel cold. Likewise, the antique desk, painted white with a cut-to-fit glass top, infuses a personal and pretty aura. The simple sofa and glass coffee table make for an inviting seating area, while the pillows and throw help soften a highly utilitarian space.

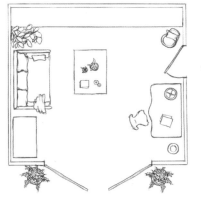

floor plan
This is a seriously high-function layout, ideal for someone who likes to move around while working. The desk nestles in one corner, while the sofa and coffee table on the opposite side provide a place to relax— or just get a new perspective. The room-width open shelving is super-accessible.

Office of Kelly
Rutherford, *actor*

the style.
hollywood
glamour

PASTELS WITH DRAMA Pale blue on one wall and the floor seems
more Tiffany than baby-boy here because of the luxe furnishings. White tones
it down, accentuates the architecture and brightens the room. Black frames
cut the palette's sweetness.

WALLS   CHAIRS   STOOLS   RUG

FEMININE FURNITURE There's nothing high-tech or work-y in here.
A Chippendale desk chair and a pair of velvet club chairs read more like
something from the living room. A glass-top desk with no drawers could be a
dining-room table. Pagoda shades on the lamps are romantic and bedroom-y,
as is the silk rug.

MAXIMALISM REINED IN WITH SYMMETRY Even though
the desk is packed with fancy objects and the walls with pictures and
swatches, the room feels calm, thanks to the placement of the lamps and the
club chairs. A bit of structure gives license to go a little wild in the details.

ART THAT SIGNALS ELEGANCE A wall of iconic imagery—
mostly pages torn from books—makes a graphic composition. The floral mural
behind gives the nook a subtle depth.

floor plan
The large desk, with chair
facing outward into the room,
dominates the space—and
makes clear who's boss. Two
large upholstered chairs echo
the lamps and balance the
slighter desk chair. The file
cabinet is tucked discreetly into
a small nook opposite the sofa.

Office of Mary McDonald,
interior designer

the big piece: desks

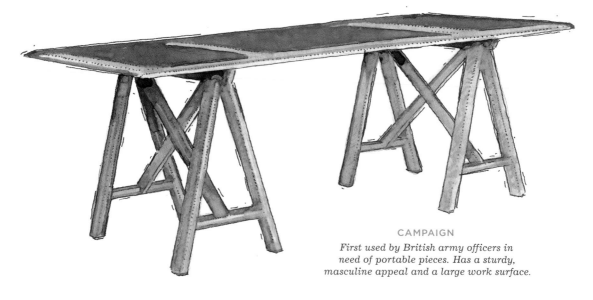

CAMPAIGN

*First used by British army officers in
need of portable pieces. Has a sturdy,
masculine appeal and a large work surface.*

CUBBY

*Streamlined version of a conventional model
with drawers. George Nelson's mid-century
classic is shown here, but more traditional styles
are available. Lean and airy.*

SECRETARY

*Tall cabinet with fold-down desktop dates
to the early 18th century. Its verticality makes it
practical for a small room.*

CLASSIC WITH DRAWERS

Symmetrical kneehole style dates back to the reign of Louis XIV. Serious workhorse with lots of storage, but can be decorative.

PARSONS

Versatile 1930s icon—width of the legs equals thickness of the top. Crisp, clean, modern.

TRADITIONAL

Reminiscent of an 18th-century English sideboard. Leggy and feminine with a rounded opening. Pretty enough for any room.

DINING TABLE

Unconventional yet still functional. Can float in the room.

FILE CABINETS + TOP

No frills and totally utilitarian. Cute-ify with colorful cabinets and a nice surface.

INSTANT EXPERT:
buying a desk

THE RIGHT PIECE Your desk might live in a dedicated office space, or it might have to double as your dining table. Consider the room it will be in when choosing a style. If it will go in your bedroom, a guest room or the living room, select a piece that is suited to those rooms, doesn't seem too office-y and will look good when not in use.

how to mix & match

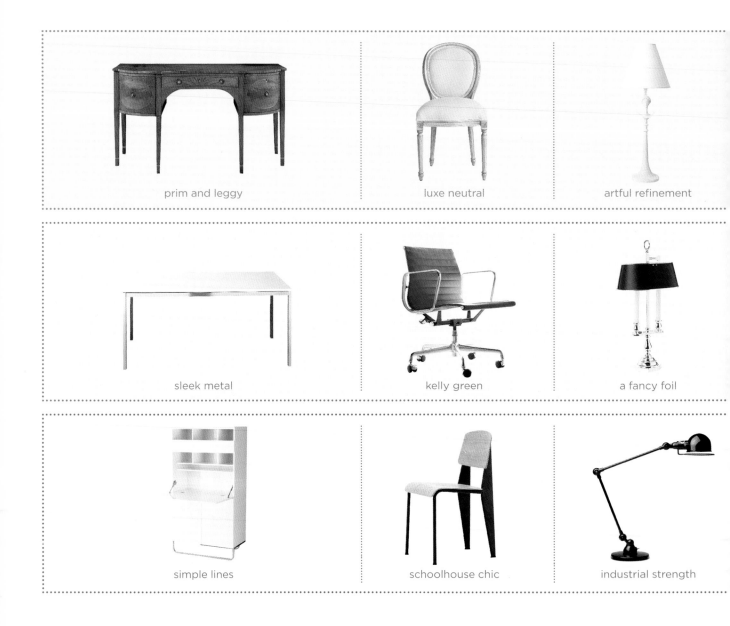

prim and leggy

luxe neutral

artful refinement

sleek metal

kelly green

a fancy foil

simple lines

schoolhouse chic

industrial strength

delicate brass

lighthearted monogram

These subtly feminine and formal elements look like they belong to an **uptown lady decorator**. The antique-y wood desk sets the tone, while a circle-back seat in a lighter finish and a sculptural lamp soften the stateliness. The neutral palette keeps the genteel style quietly understated.

crisp piping

traditional stamp

The contrasting palette of white, green and black unifies designs inspired by different eras, with an overall **clean and preppy** effect. The modern desk and utilitarian Eames chair make the elaborate repro French *bouillote* lamp an elegant surprise.

delicate rusticity

organic pattern

The mid-century Jean Prouvé chair epitomizes the **warm yet cool** look created by a French workshop lamp, woven storage baskets and floral stationery, with a sharp white secretary as backdrop.

very important tips

chairs

FORM + FUNCTION If you use your home office full-time, find a chair that provides support and style. A modern ergonomic chair can be chic in a traditionally furnished space—think antique desk paired with Aeron chair. The opposite can be true too.

SMOOTH SITTING Casters on office chairs are great, but make sure they're given an even plane to roll across.

lighting

FORM + FUNCTION No need to stress about matching eras with the rest of the room. A modern task lamp looks surprisingly good in a traditional setting. Decorative lamps may be lovely, but they generally don't offer enough focused light to be the sole source for this utilitarian environment.

BULBS Good lighting is key here. CFLs (compact fluorescent lights), though a great energy-saving alternative to incandescents, may not be intense enough for your work space. LEDs (light-emitting diodes) are a better fit for the office. These energy-efficient bulbs are extremely bright and long-lasting.

storage/tech support

FILE CABINETS They don't have to be ugly! In a vibrant
color (like the green above) or metallic (far left), cabinets
can be a happy decor element. Lateral cabinets are generally
more stable than vertical ones (check that the unit is
counterweighted so it doesn't topple when open and full), and
they supply an extra work surface. If you prefer your files out
of sight, hide them in a closet or under a skirted table.

WIRE MANAGEMENT Until the day tech goes
completely wireless, the best we can do is keep cords as
orderly as possible. A cord organizer will help avoid the big
tangle. Also, if you use a desktop computer, position the desk
against the wall to hide wires. A laptop offers the freedom to
float the desk elsewhere in the room.

accessories

KITTING IT OUT WITH PANACHE To put the
finishing touches on your office, be thoughtful down to the
last accessory. Beauty counts. Go for some form of unity by
limiting your choices to a basic palette and/or style—all pop
color, say, or all earthy modern.

THE CHECKLIST A place for everything allows everything
to return to its place. And having supplies you need at hand
ensures no scrambling around searching for tape or a pen.

- [ ] storage baskets/
      boxes
- [ ] organizing trays
- [ ] wastepaper basket
- [ ] pens, pencils & cup
- [ ] clock

- [ ] stapler, tape
      dispenser & scissors
- [ ] paper clips & holder
- [ ] mouse pad
- [ ] bulletin board &
      pushpins

decorating tricks

FRAMING A DESK with a whimsical canopy and curtains makes finances a little more fun.

A DESK PLACED IN FRONT OF A BOOKCASE can work when wall space isn't available.

DISGUISING A FILE CABINET with "chinoiserie" (really just vintage fabric enlarged on a photocopier) is a quirky reinvention of a decorator favorite.

AN EMBELLISHED CLOTH SKIRT attached with Velcro provides easy access to high (but hidden) tech.

RIG UP A DESK with filing cabinets and a laminate top—the all-white scheme keeps it from looking like a DIY project.

more decorating tricks

SCULPTURAL STOOLS AND BENCHES are attractive mini workstations.

A LUSH WALLPAPER is an antidote to an antiseptic office.

FROUFROU CHAIRS are a surprising pairing with an industrial table.

AN EXTRA-LONG DESK mounted on the wall accommodates more than one person in slim confines.

BACK-TO-BACK TABLES make an impromptu partners desk in a space that needs to fit two.

small-space solutions

NO ROOM FOR AN OFFICE?
Try a table behind the sofa or
somewhere in the living room.

USE NEGLECTED AREAS—a secretary and a shelf carve out a work nook under the stairs.

FLOOR SPACE IS OVERRATED! A desk, a chair, bookshelves and a daybed all fit in this tiny room, which can double as guest quarters.

A SECRETARY DESK easily hides its official duties (just flip up the "Murphy" tabletop) and reads as pretty furniture.

TURN A CLOSET INTO A SECRET WORK ZONE with a makeshift desk plus a shelf for storage. Close the doors after 5 P.M.

finishing touches

ART BELONGS IN THE
OFFICE TOO—layer it and hang
it for an energetic composition.

A PERSONAL ASSORTMENT of accessories adds a little joy to paying bills.

COLOR-CODED BINDERS lend cohesiveness to storage space.

GLAMOUR IS IN THE DETAILS—uniformly polished desk accessories telegraph "I've got it together."

WALL-TO-WALL INSPIRATION images create an artful collage.

207

the domino effect

the starting point

"We had a spare room in our new apartment—finally. I wanted to make it into a personal haven that felt like another realm from the sunny apartment I share with my husband and kids."

DARA CAPONIGRO
domino *style director*

existing furniture

"When we moved in, I had six of these bookcases. I decided to stack them as a group, so the room would feel more like a library than an office. To fill the wall, I ordered three more. This desk had been my bedside table, but now that I had extra space, it became my desk."

"The objects I love most have some kind of meaning to me—either a friend designed them or they came from a trip and have a memory attached. I collected these feathers when I was little."

"A sculpture made by my mother."

sentimental pieces

"This was our living-room chair from the '60s. Having grown up in a modernist house, I always need something modern in a room."

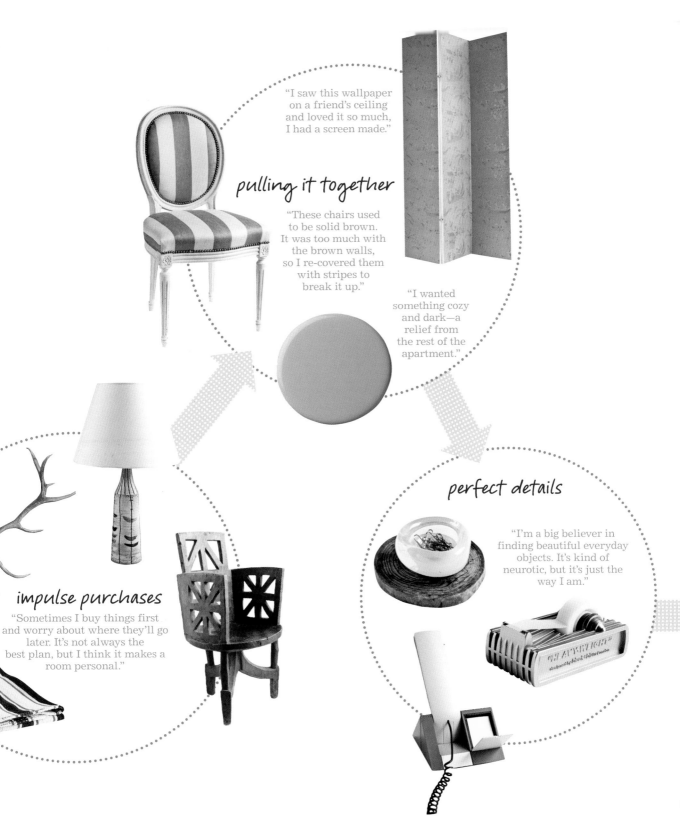

"I saw this wallpaper on a friend's ceiling and loved it so much, I had a screen made."

pulling it together

"These chairs used to be solid brown. It was too much with the brown walls, so I re-covered them with stripes to break it up."

"I wanted something cozy and dark—a relief from the rest of the apartment."

perfect details

"I'm a big believer in finding beautiful everyday objects. It's kind of neurotic, but it's just the way I am."

impulse purchases

"Sometimes I buy things first and worry about where they'll go later. It's not always the best plan, but I think it makes a room personal."

my office

"I wanted my office to look lived-in—even a little messy—because I grew up in a very neat house."

—DARA CAPONIGRO

CHAPTER NINE

the kids' room

the style:
urbane cowboy

SLEEPY PALETTE WITH A SHOCK OF RED Dusty-green walls and vintage-inspired curtains set a soft, subdued tone. The nightstand and box-spring covers pick up on the crimson in the curtains, providing a jolt of energy. A dark hardwood floor fits in with the rustic, home-on-the range vibe.

WALLS   CURTAINS   RUGS   COVERLETS

A HODGEPODGE OF PATTERN An adventurer's spirit runs throughout the similarly scaled mix of fabrics. The Navajo-style rugs tie into the Old West theme of the curtains, while a swanky zebra print on the headboards offers an element of surprise.

COMPLEMENTARY SHAPES A subtle wave design in the coverlets accentuates the beds' feminine silhouettes; the curvy bed frames balance out the boyishness.

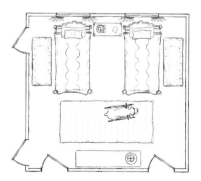

floor plan
Twin beds in a single occupant's space are tailor-made for sleepovers. Placing the beds side by side against the windows establishes a pleasing symmetry.

Kid's room of Vesta
Fort, decorator

the style:
mod baby

HIGH CONTRAST A single black wall stands in stark relief to white walls and the yellow-and-white striped ceiling. The *noir* dresser blends into the backdrop, creating a chic yet theatrical visual effect.

WALL   CEILING   WALLS   BEDDING

MODERN AMUSEMENT Circus-y stripes painted on the ceiling give the room a flipped-upside-down curiosity. The graphic lines assist a simple mobile in keeping a baby's eyes busy before bedtime.

TIMELESS CLASSICS A crib that is both aesthetically pleasing and functional is a wise investment that will last generations. Likewise, a tall, solid dresser with beautiful gold detail and interesting pulls can reside in the room even after the child goes to college.

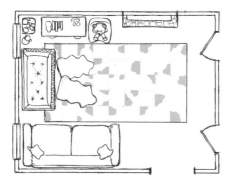

floor plan
Placed between two windows, the crib is shielded from direct sun but still benefits from natural light. The center of the room remains open and airy to accommodate play, while a sofa gives adults a comfortable place to sit.

Kid's room of Jenna Lyons and Vincent Mazeau, *creative director and artist*

the style:
plush & pretty

ENCAPSULATING COLOR Pairing lavender walls with cornflower-blue curtains and headboard gives the quaint room an all-encompassing elegance. White bedding and accents exert a crispness on what might otherwise feel overly fussy.

WALLPAPER CURTAINS BED FABRIC

LAYERED SOPHISTICATION The faint floral of the wallpaper adds interest without overwhelming. Cotton-velvet upholstery and voluptuous floor-length Indian silk curtains (the rods are longer than the width of the frame, feigning larger windows) create an air of luxury in a tight space.

POSH BUT PRACTICAL LIGHTING A simple swing-arm wall sconce frees up surface area on the bedside table. Also, to temper the frippery, an undulated modern orb hangs overhead.

LAVISH COMFORT This enormous tufted sleigh bed forges an ultra-cozy setting that makes other furniture seem unnecessary. It has an architectural, room-within-a-room allure.

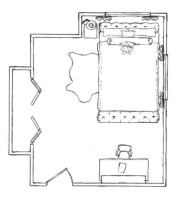

floor plan
The big bed is the dominant element in this small room, transforming the space into a giant spot for lounging. A wide closet and wall-mounted shelving above the desk provide ample storage.

Kid's room of Sharon
Simonaire, *interior designer*

the big piece: kids' beds

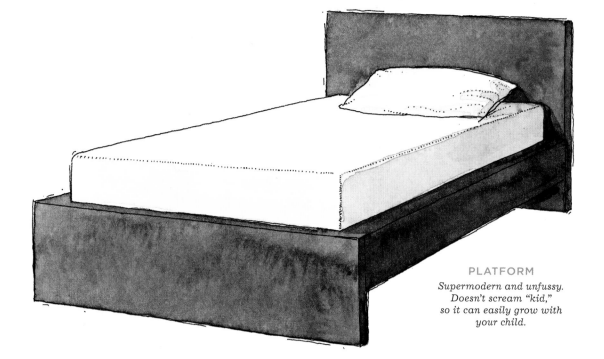

PLATFORM

*Supermodern and unfussy.
Doesn't scream "kid,"
so it can easily grow with
your child.*

BUNK BED

*Space-saving and always a hit. Comes in
modern and traditional styles.*

TRUNDLE

*Dates back to when mistresses and their maids
slept in the same room. Great for sleepovers.*

CANOPY

Grown-up yet girly. Creates a little haven, with or without a fabric canopy. This one piece makes a room feel decorated.

UPHOLSTERED

Luxurious and grown-up. Makes for a cozy bedtime story.

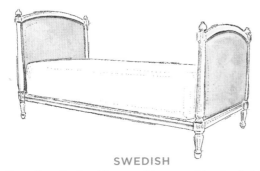

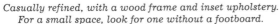

SWEDISH

Casually refined, with a wood frame and inset upholstery. For a small space, look for one without a footboard.

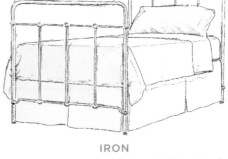

IRON

Classic and romantic. Often available painted.

COTTAGE

Charming and unpretentious. Cute in a pair.

SPOOL

A 19th-century, turned-wood design. Painted, it's sweet in a girl's room; a natural wood finish is great for boys. Nice in a guest room later.

how to mix & match

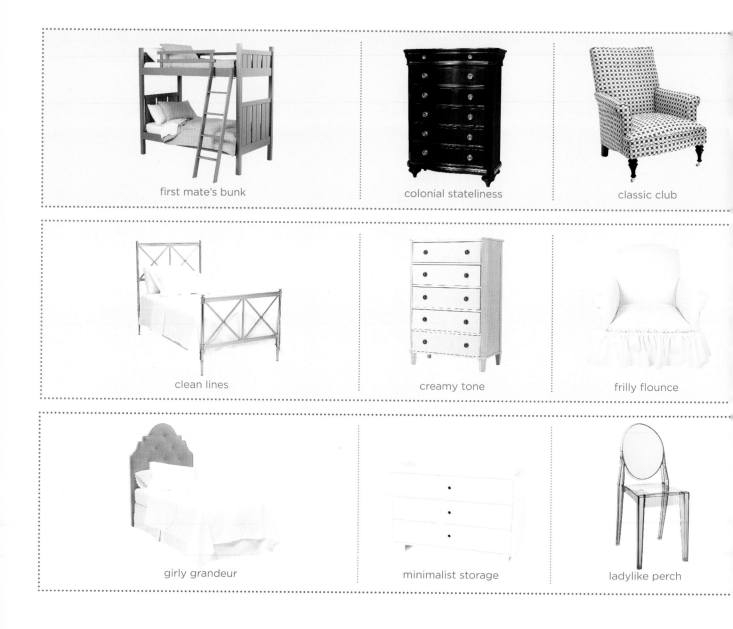

first mate's bunk

colonial stateliness

classic club

clean lines

creamy tone

frilly flounce

girly grandeur

minimalist storage

ladylike perch

seafaring chandelier

rugged rope

Tailored, traditional elements combine with upscale maritime accents to impart a **preppy nautical** mood. The youthful pop of pattern on a grown-up chair links to the green bunk.

organic lace

baroque touch

Silver, cream and straw hues connect the more boxy, straightforward shapes to a cozy ruffled chair and a scalloped chandelier for a **tidy, neutral and feminine** feel. Crocheted detailing and a hint of print add texture.

fun & funky

earthy texture

A tufted headboard, a witty take on a Louis XV chair and a Chinese paper lantern are fanciful accoutrements for a **modern-day princess**. The sleek bureau and nubby basket keep the look from going over the top.

very important tips

paint/fabric

SELECTING A COLOR Don't be afraid of a sophisticated palette—try a hue you'd want in your own room. If you do subscribe to the prescribed pink-for-girls-blue-for-boys approach, consider variations. A vibrant fuchsia or blue-gray are refreshing alternatives to powdery pastels. The key— particularly for older kids—is to select color combinations that have longevity and suit a range of styles.

BEDDING AS DECOR Graphic sheet sets and duvets are a great affordable way to liven up a basic room. They help set the tone: Dainty florals have a sweet vibe while a geometric pattern feels punchy and modern. More interchangeable than furniture or window treatments, bed linens can also better accommodate evolving tastes.

DURABLE MATERIALS When outfitting a child's room, pick fabrics that can withstand wear and tear. If something is white, make sure it's machine-washable. Cotton duck, twill and canvas are all low-maintenance and built to last.

furniture

PIECES TO GROW WITH Unless you plan on constantly redecorating, choose heirloom-worthy pieces that children will come to appreciate. A beautiful armoire is practical for housing everything from toys to clothing. And if a basic rocking chair cramps your style, there are more sophisticated options, like the Eames rocker (above). Furniture likely to adapt over time—a crib that converts into a bed, a bureau repurposed as a changing table—is more cost-effective. Think about what's normally found in other parts of the house that could function in a child's room; a large modern coffee table, for instance, makes a versatile post for art projects and tea parties.

ALL-IMPORTANT LIGHTING Children should have access to an abundance of light: bright overheads, task lamps for desks, reading lamps for bedside tables and even night-lights, so toes aren't stubbed on the way to the bathroom.

GROUND EFFECTS A rug provides insulation for hardwood floors, extra padding for busy knees and another blast of color or pattern.

storage

THE BIG IDEAS Children have tons of stuff—now figure out where it's all going. Space permitting, plot out where to use organizational pieces: a tall chest of drawers, a bookshelf, shelving, cabinets, etc. Take advantage of the room's architecture. If there's a recess or indentation in the wall, install shelving (as above). But keep the height of the child in mind. Toys, books and puzzles should be within arm's reach, so he or she can pull items out and put them away. Other, more decorative bits can live higher up.

MIDDLE GROUND While labeled boxes, bins and baskets may seem semi-neurotic, they actually preserve sanity. Everything from superheroes and dinosaurs to model modes of transportation can have its own designated spot. This will encourage organization and make for easy after-play cleanup that kids can be involved in.

THINK SMALL Take advantage of all usable space. Stow off-season clothes and out-of-favor playthings under the bed. Put up a bulletin board for loose papers and memorabilia. Hang peg hooks (low!) inside a closet door for jerseys, hats and belts. Same goes for behind the bedroom door.

baby room

HEALTHY CHOICES A lot of children's furniture is, unfortunately, made with toxins like formaldehyde. Scrutinize material information and, when possible, go for natural alternatives, like wood, sea grass, sisal, hemp or jute. Many paint companies offer water-based, low- and non-VOC (Volatile Organic Compounds) products, which won't release harmful gases into the air. And an ever-growing variety of eco bed linens and fabric (bamboo, organic cotton, hemp, etc.) for curtains and upholstery is ripe for the picking. Even mattresses come stuffed with all-organic filling and wool casings.

A NOTE ON THEMES Keep in mind that overly juvenile, cartoon-y motifs aren't necessarily going to make children happy. A well-decorated space sans theme, which leaves room for the imagination, will appeal to everyone in the family.

decorating tricks

CARPET TILES can be pieced together into a pattern (and readily replaced if need be).

PINK DOESN'T HAVE TO BE GIRLY when it's offset with a black rug.

WHIMSICAL WALLPAPER on the ceiling gives kids something fun to look at when they're lying in bed.

REINVENT A BEAUTIFUL CHEST into a changing table by topping it with a snug cushion.

LONG, FULL CURTAINS distinguish a sleeping alcove as its own special space.

more decorating tricks

GRASS-CLOTH WALLS lend warm sophistication to a child's room and serve as a massive bulletin board for artwork.

SET OFF A TRADITIONAL PINK with bright orange to take a girl's room from toddler to tween.

SIMPLE HOOKS keep jackets and bags off the ground.

CHALKBOARD PAINT is lower-commitment than a real board, but just as fun.

A COOL STENCIL in a bright color becomes abstract art for the modern kid.

small-space solutions

A SLEEPING LOFT has indoor treehouse appeal and frees up valuable real estate below.

ORK CLOTHES

The poacher's cham to blend in with his was the secret of

IF ALL THE KIDS BUNK IN ONE ROOM, another bedroom can be dedicated to play.

ONE GIANT GUEST ROOM with lots of beds doesn't limit your invitations.

REAPPROPRIATE A HALL CLOSET if there's no proper storage in the nursery.

CREATE INSTANT PRIVACY with curtains on a track.

finishing touches

CURATE A COLLAGE of framed and taped-up photos, postcards and souvenirs that highlight a passion or hobby.

SPELLING OUT A CHILD'S NAME in bold, mismatched letters will make him feel like a rock star.

A CORK WALL allows for rotating gallery exhibits.

A FABRIC-COVERED BULLETIN BOARD with crisscrossed ribbon lends some order to a chaotic collection.

LET ONE BIG IMAGE be the room's focal point. A giant map of the world is perfect—colorful and educational!

the domino effect

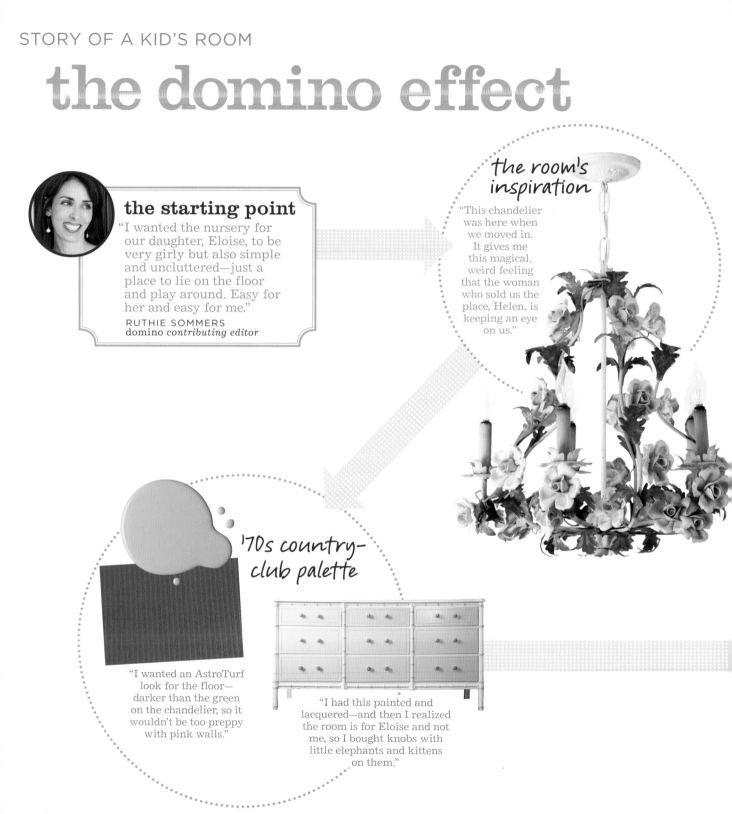

the starting point

"I wanted the nursery for our daughter, Eloise, to be very girly but also simple and uncluttered—just a place to lie on the floor and play around. Easy for her and easy for me."

RUTHIE SOMMERS
domino *contributing editor*

the room's inspiration

"This chandelier was here when we moved in. It gives me this magical, weird feeling that the woman who sold us the place, Helen, is keeping an eye on us."

'70s country-club palette

"I wanted an AstroTurf look for the floor—darker than the green on the chandelier, so it wouldn't be too preppy with pink walls."

"I had this painted and lacquered—and then I realized the room is for Eloise and not me, so I bought knobs with little elephants and kittens on them."

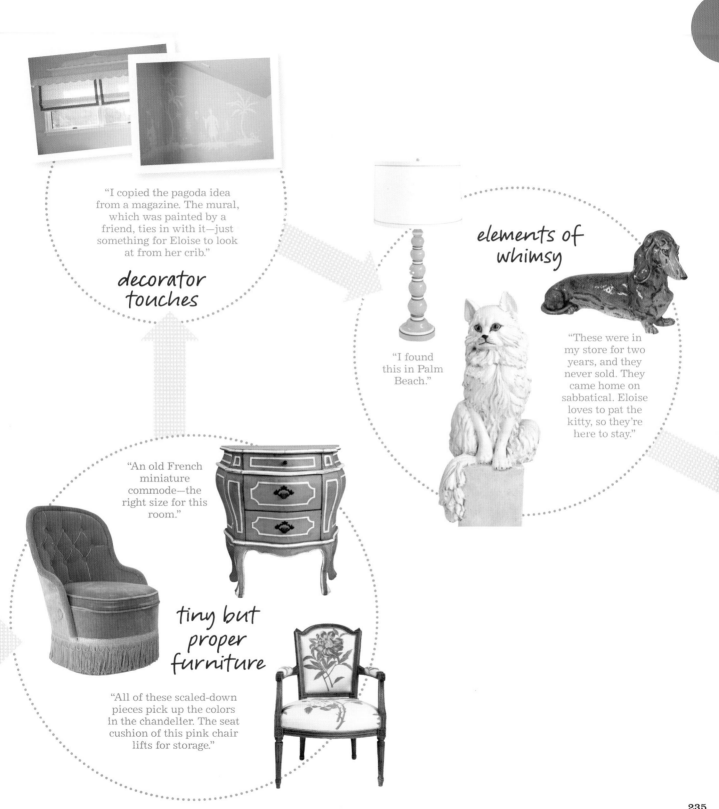

"I copied the pagoda idea from a magazine. The mural, which was painted by a friend, ties in with it—just something for Eloise to look at from her crib."

decorator touches

elements of whimsy

"I found this in Palm Beach."

"These were in my store for two years, and they never sold. They came home on sabbatical. Eloise loves to pat the kitty, so they're here to stay."

"An old French miniature commode—the right size for this room."

tiny but proper furniture

"All of these scaled-down pieces pick up the colors in the chandelier. The seat cushion of this pink chair lifts for storage."

my kid's room

"When I'm in here, I always feel so appreciative. My daughter is what I see most in this room, not loads of toys, photos and accoutrements—just her. Pink for healthy, pink for girly." —RUTHIE SOMMERS

the decorators' handbook

a guide to window treatments and upholstery

windows: curtains

CURTAIN STYLES

DOUBLE PANEL
The most popular style, a pair of panels bracketing a window establishes symmetry and order.

good to know: If your room—or your window—is small, double panels can overwhelm. Pick a lightweight fabric that's not too voluminous, or opt for a single panel.

SINGLE PANEL
A single panel works well in snug spaces or when windows are closely set. A dynamic sweep of fabric caught to one side with a tieback is romantic, while a simple straight-hung panel in front of the window is casual.

good to know: Can look prim tied to one side, but done in a sheer fabric, it's elegant.

PANELS WITH VALANCE
A soft fabric valance gives plain panels a more romantic quality. Taut or shirred, it can run straight across at the bottom, or can undulate.

good to know: Unpretentious solids, like linen and cotton can foil the potential fussiness. A valance alone (without panels) can add softness to an uncovered window.

PANELS WITH PELMET
Enclosing the top of the curtain in a structured frame, a pelmet lends a well-mannered air.

good to know: Not for windows that open inward. Pelmets themselves are often adorned to highlight their shape.

STACKED CURTAINS
The epitome of boutique-hotel chic, a voluminous cascade of floor-to-ceiling fabric gives a sumptuously clean look that's surprisingly minimalist when rendered in gauzy fabrics. This enveloping style fosters the illusion of bigger windows and mellows the lines of a stark room.

good to know: This is a lot of fabric, so keep it light.

CAFÉ CURTAINS
Hung at a window's midpoint or above, café curtains add a hint of color and flounce where full-blown coverage isn't needed.

good to know: Although not the best for tempering sunlight, café curtains effectively screen views when hung at just the right spot.

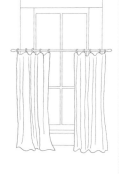

FABRICS

COTTON
pros: Incredibly versatile and easy to clean.

cons: Some stiffer cottons don't have enough give for graceful draping styles.

LINEN
pros: The open weave provides texture and refinement. Looks substantial lined but can also be left as is to play light off the fabric's openness.

cons: Some linen is dry-clean only, so not well suited for rooms or windows that get lots of dirt and dust.

SILK
pros: Refined yet light, silk catches a breeze and billows beautifully.

cons: Often too sheer to screen light and views very well, unless it's lined.

SHEERS
pros: Cut glare while still filtering light, thus great for where you need a bit of privacy but don't want the hassle of opening and shutting curtains all the time.

cons: The translucent weave won't block light, so pair with a heavier curtain in a bedroom. (See p. 245.)

VELVET
pros: Velvet's richness feels luxurious. Its plush weight also offers privacy and good insulation from drafts and sunlight.

cons: Can be expensive and formal—and a little heavy for warm climates.

WOOL
pros: Wool drapes beautifully and is strong enough to support heavy embellishments like fringe and tassels.

cons: While summer-weight wool is all-seasonal, its moisture absorbency makes it ill-suited to beach environments. Wool is dry-clean only.

CURTAIN HEADINGS

POLE POCKET

A straightforward option in which the curtain rod slips through a channel in the top of the panel, creating a gathered effect without the use of pleats or rings.

good to know: It can be hard to move the fabric back and forth, so this is best for stationary curtains.

PENCIL PLEAT

Bestowing instant posh, these tight, even pleats create a nicely refined shirring. Great for stacked curtains.

good to know: The look leans pretty debonair, so restrict it to fairly upscale confines.

FLOPPY

A fold of fabric at the top, which forms a composed ruffle and draws the eye up, brings a little frill without going overboard.

good to know: This pretty treatment is somewhat lighthearted, so best in cottons and linens.

GROMMET

The rod threads through grommets, making rings unnecessary. These circular metal perforations read as fun and modern.

good to know: If you're prone to casually pushing curtains open and shut, grommets may prove a bit challenging.

PINCH PLEAT

A succession of gathered pleats at the top of the curtain unfurls in a graceful cascade, creating a sense of movement. Double pleats (above) are more tailored, while triples yield extra volume.

good to know: Also called French pleats, this tailoring works well with heavy or light fabrics, telegraphing folds from top to bottom.

SOFT INVERTED PLEAT

These elegant pleats are made by folding the fabric back, rather than forward.

good to know: Crisper fabrics will highlight the tailoring.

TIE-TOP

Tied directly onto rings or a rod, these charming panels are girly fastened in bows. In knots, they're less feminine.

good to know: These tops let you adjust how closely the curtain hangs to the rod—leave a bit loose for a lived-in boho look.

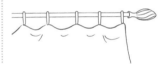

PLAIN HEADING

One of the most common options, these understated panels hang flat and require the least fabric.

good to know: With no ties or tabs to attach the panels to a curtain rod, these usually affix with clip-on rings, which should be evenly spaced to avoid looking messy.

TINY SOFT PINCH PLEAT

Achieved by pinching together the very top of the fabric panel, these delicate pleats are looser than pinch pleats and more bohemian.

good to know: These require less yardage than the more structured pinch pleat.

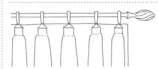

BOX PLEAT

These big, flat folds convey a custom quality that's equal parts Dorothy Draper and old-school Hollywood glam.

good to know: This classic style veers a bit traditional. Also, because the pleats fold the fabric under itself, wild patterns might not work.

HIDDEN CURTAIN DETAILS

LINING

An extra layer of fabric backing gives curtains body and makes them substantial. While many fabrics—like cotton or silk—drape better when lined, your choice is also a matter of aesthetics. You can use unlined linen to make a fancy living room less formal or opt for lined velvet panels to step up a laid-back bedroom.

INTERLINING

Interlining is a hidden panel sewn between the lining and the fabric you actually see in the room. It ensures that the curtain is opaque and adds weight, so that the curtain falls nicely.

WEIGHTS

Stitched into the hem, weights help fabrics hang with more heft and keep curtains in place so you don't have to futz with them.

windows: curtains, cont'd

CURTAIN LENGTH

BRUSHING THE FLOOR

Imparts a crisp and tailored look, like a well-cut suit. Curtain panels that just touch the floor offer a perfect canvas for edging or borders. This structured style is best with heavier fabrics like velvet and lined cotton. It will, however, call attention to crooked floors (which can be disguised by a bit more length).

BREAKING THE FLOOR

A little softer than curtains that just brush the floor, those that break onto the floor by an inch or two are relaxed and voluptuous. Going a bit longer also allows some room for imperfect measuring.

POOLING AT THE FLOOR

More than two inches of extra curtain tracing the floor imbues a lush, romantic sensibility. Any trim along the bottom will be less visible since the curtains will scrunch up a bit.

A NOTE ABOUT SHORT CURTAINS

Short curtains are tricky to pull off, unless they're café-style. They can work when their bottoms are hitting something, like a radiator cover or a bookcase, but can seem out-of-date if they're just dangling in the air. For a window that can't take full-length curtains, a shade is often the perfect solution.

PELMETS

A pelmet is a wood box cut to shape, sometimes padded and usually covered with fabric. Curvy profiles are more traditional. Pelmets can also be made entirely of finished wood, which can help counteract a room with fabric overload.

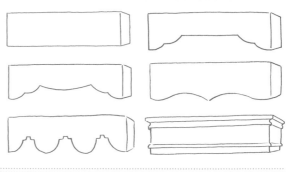

BORDERS & TRIMS

CURTAIN BORDERS

Contrasting fabric or tape defining the bottom, sides and/or top of the panel breaks up an expanse of material—and can tie colors in to the rest of the room. Often only the inside edge and bottom have borders. *good to know:* An inset border a few inches from the edge is less graphic and more refined.

CURTAIN TRIMS

Fringe, pom-poms ruffles or other embellishments (known collectively to pros as passementerie) along the edge of a curtain bring a polished quality that's more delicate than a bold border. A great way to customize off-the-shelf panels. *good to know:* Trims can go on the inside edge only, along the bottom only or all around a panel.

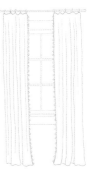

TIEBACKS

FABRIC

A strip of cloth that hooks to the wall confers a finished quality. Mount low for a dramatic swoop of fabric or high to rein in panels tightly.

ROPE

While loosely draped curtains are always stylish, a rope tieback, attached to the wall by a hook, offers a sophisticated, European look.

METAL BRACKET

Hardware in brass, iron or bronze is the easiest way to pull back curtains—especially those you're constantly opening and closing.

ROSETTE

Rosettes can be unfussy or ornate and come in a variety of materials (brass, bronze, even mercury glass). Curtains simply drape over them.

HANGING OPTIONS

HOW HIGH?
Curtains often look best mounted a few inches above the top of the molding. Hang even higher to downplay crooked windows or create the illusion of higher ceilings. Keep rod placement in mind when buying curtains. Measure from rod to floor, accounting for length of rings and how much you want curtains to break. When in doubt, overestimate. You can hem them later.

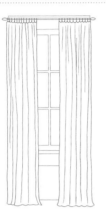

HOW WIDE?
Rods work well when they continue at least a few inches beyond the window molding. Just how far depends on your desired look and how much daylight you want. To maximize light, extend the rod at least 10" beyond the frame on each side. Hanging extra-wide also makes small windows seem bigger.

CUSTOM VS. READY-MADE

Like a bespoke suit, custom drapes just fit better. Consider this, especially if you're particular about your curtains or if your windows don't conform to standard sizes. Custom allows for more variation. Ready-mades might lack that tailored appeal, but they're less expensive, don't require long lead times—and if what you receive isn't what you had in mind, you can return them. If you're getting curtains made, have the fabric laundered first—and remember that gathering, pleats and elongated styles all mean more yardage.

CURTAIN-ROD STYLES

ROD WITH FINIAL
These come in a variety of materials, most commonly wood and metal. Different metals have different moods—brass is traditional, iron is understated. Wood rods add warmth. Paint them to highlight a color in the room.

RETURN ROD
These U-shaped rods curve into the wall, obviating the need for finials. Ideal for rooms that demand complete darkness, since the fabric wraps around the side of the windows to seal out light. They're streamlined and less fussy than other choices.

CABLE ROD
Cables are simple to install, anchoring right into the wall with screws. You can adjust the tension so the cable hangs tightly or a little slack for a more relaxed look.

CEILING TRACK
Somewhat tricky to install—it's best to enlist a professional, especially if you want it flush-mounted (flat to the ceiling)—a ceiling track generally entails custom-designed curtains, which clip on with hooks. But once in place, a track is effortless to use and takes full advantage of ceiling height.

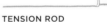

SIDE-WALL MOUNT
Although curtain rods are usually mounted on the same wall as the window, you can instead anchor them to perpendicular side walls for a dramatic sweep of uninterrupted curtain.

TENSION ROD
The easiest and least expensive option (also the least finished-looking), these can be picked up for just a few dollars at the hardware store and slipped inside the window frame. They're best with pole-pocket curtains and won't hold heavy drapes.

CURTAIN-ROD ACCESSORIES

RING WITH EYE
Most curtains attach to rings via curtain hooks. The curtain hook threads through the eye of the ring.

RING WITHOUT EYE
The poshest curtains are stitched directly onto eyeless rings, making professional cleaning a must. These rings also work for tie-tops.

RING WITH CLIP
These affix to curtains like clip-on earrings, and can convert any piece of fabric into a curtain.

FINIALS
Adorning the ends of rods like jewelry, finials are an effortless way to add style.

BRACKET
These support the rod and are typically mounted near its ends. Sometimes a center bracket is needed to help hold an extralong rod.

windows: shades

SHADE & BLIND STYLES

ROLLER
These simple shades roll up via a spring-load mechanism or chain. Roller shades come in a variety of styles and perform expertly in snug confines where cascades of fabric or weighty curtain rods would overwhelm. You can upgrade off-the-shelf versions with trim or decorative pulls.

MATCHSTICK
The natural material adds a warm quality. These blinds temper strong daylight without totally obliterating it. Hung solo, they're casual. Paired with a fancier curtain, they become almost dressy.

WOOD VENETIAN
Made of stacked slats, these blinds tilt to any angle to reduce the light while letting in views (or vice versa). You can often customize the color of the "ladder tape" that runs top to bottom. Unlike paper or fabric blinds, which are easy to vacuum, these can be challenging to clean.

FLAT ROMAN
Roman shades are formed from fabric folds that stack neatly as they're opened. Streamlined and architectural, they lend themselves well to having borders.

RELAXED ROMAN
These operate the same way as the classic flat-fold version, rising via a pulley mechanism. Softer than a flat roman, they feature a subtle, voluminous drape and a design that can show off patterned fabric.

PLEATED ROMAN
Similar to a standard roman shade, this style is distinguished by horizontal pleats, which highlight detailing even when lowered.

LONDON
These hang with a dashing swag of fabric at the bottom. A great ornamental style for windows that don't need shades to be opened and shut frequently.

BALLOON
These literally "balloon" out in little puffs of fabric, bestowing a sweetness that can lean a bit saccharine. Keep it pared-back by choosing a plain fabric or a subtle print.

FABRICS

SHEER VS. OPAQUE
The sheerer a fabric, the lighter the look and the more daylight it will admit, whereas heavier fabrics help diminish street noise or drafts but can darken a room.

good to know: If you need to screen views but want ample light, pick an opaque weave in a pale color, like white or cream.

PATTERN VS. SOLID
Just like with upholstery, a patterned shade is livelier than a solid. Patterns work best on styles without pleats. Also consider how light shining through may make the pattern more diffuse. Using a lining can keep it visible.

good to know: Fancy styles like balloon shades and london shades can be played down with solid fabrics—they have plenty of embellishment on their own.

PLACEMENT OF THE PATTERN
Whether you're planning to sew your own curtains or have them custom-made, center the pattern.

good to know: If your chosen fabric features an oversize motif or large repeat (see p. 246), account for extra yardage so the pattern can align correctly on the shade.

BLACKOUT
In rooms where you want complete darkness, there are a few ways to go. Many off-the-shelf roller blinds are available as blackout shades. If you're ordering custom, you can request blackout lining.

MOUNTING OPTIONS

INSIDE MOUNT

The most common mounting method, this works well with any style shade and nets the cleanest look.

good to know: Hang shades so they skim the inside of the window moldings—close enough to block out light, but with enough space to raise and lower without catching. Can make small windows seem even smaller.

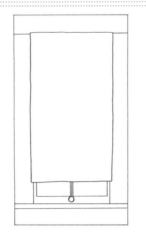

OUTSIDE MOUNT

A good option for when you want to create the illusion of wider windows, cover unattractive frames or seal out daylight completely.

good to know: To make your ceiling appear higher, hang outside-mounted shades several inches above the window frame (remember to measure from where you plan to hang to the top of your sill). When you raise a high-mounted shade, just remember not to roll it up past the top of the window.

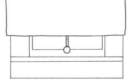

CONSIDER LEAVING WINDOWS BARE:

• When you want to accentuate a drop-dead view in a public room, like the living or dining room.

• When you want to highlight elaborately carved moldings or window frames.

• When you have a pared-down room that begs for windows that are free of frippery.

LAYERING

CURTAIN + ANOTHER CURTAIN

when to go for it: When one style can't perform all the functions you need, pick two curtains of different weights, hanging one in front of the other. This allows you to adjust for sheer coverage or total opacity.

how to make it work: Get a double rod that's designed just for this purpose.

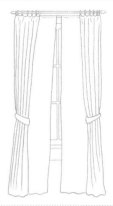

CURTAIN + VALANCE/PELMET

when to go for it: When you want to draw attention to a window or create a sense of drama.

how to make it work: It's foolproof if you use the same fabric for both curtain and valance (or pelmet).

CURTAIN + SHADE

when to go for it: In spaces like bedrooms, where you need a functional treatment but also want some decorative flair. They're less bulky than a double layer of curtains and simpler to pull off.

how to make it work: Coordinating shade and curtain fabric will be too matchy here, so choose contrasting hues or materials that still have a shared sensibility. The shade should always be inside-mounted.

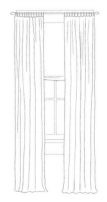

upholstery: sofas & chairs

UPHOLSTERY STYLES

TIGHT BACK, TIGHT SEAT
Streamlined and without cushions, it's pleasingly tidy and formal.

good to know: With no cushions to flip, stains can't be hidden.

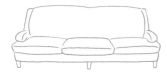

TIGHT BACK, LOOSE SEAT
Has a neat profile but is still enveloping.

good to know: The back can be a bit stiff, so consider adding throw pillows.

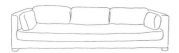

LOOSE BACK, LOOSE SEAT
Loose cushions confer a worldly but lived-in vibe and are usually more comfortable.

good to know: Make sure the cushions have enough firmness to hold their shape over time. If not, they can start to look sloppy.

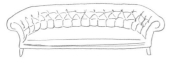

TUFTED
Button tufting spruces up a broad stretch of sofa with a quilt-like succession of stitches. Elegant and European.

good to know: You can tuft the seat, the back or both. Solids and large-scale patterns work best. Small patterns can get lost in the tufting.

SEAT CUSHIONS

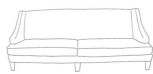

SINGLE CUSHION
pros: This streamlined look is clean and formal. It can squeeze in more people comfortably—no one has to sit on a crack between cushions—and is great for napping.

cons: In the event of stains or wear, you have only one chance to turn over the cushion.

MULTI-CUSHION
pros: Generally a bit cozier. You can move cushions around frequently, so they wear more evenly, and flip them if they become stained.

cons: Less crisp than a single cushion and can veer a bit sloppy.

CUSHION TYPES

BOX
An upholstered cushion or pillow shaped like a box, with flat sides. Welting (see next page) accentuates the squared-off form, while elaborate trims, which slip into the seams, have a tempering effect on otherwise crisp linearity.

BULLNOSE
The most common style, upholstered cushions sewn together with a single, circumnavigating seam have a slight curve to the edges. The shape is softer and a bit puffier than flat-sided box cushions, but can likewise be dressed up with welting, cords or fringe.

BUTTON
A grid of buttons can smarten up a plain box-cushion design or lend texture to a large-scale piece. Covered in the same fabric as the cushion, buttons look quite clean. Pick a contrasting color or material for a livelier effect.

THINGS TO THINK ABOUT

FILLER
There are three types of stuffing for your cushions: foam, down or a combination of the two. Foam springs back into shape after you stand up. Down filler stays squished and requires constant fluffing. The best of both worlds—and quite common—are cushions with a foam core surrounded by down.

FABRIC
Your fabric choice should suit both your frame style and your life. Account for pragmatic considerations such as how much wear the piece will be subject to—children, pets or strong sunlight should influence your choice.

PATTERN
Always consider orientation of the pattern: Most fabrics that are directional (like stripes) are upholstered vertically. Patterns are generally centered, which means buying additional yardage if your print is oversize.

REPEAT AND SIZE
The "repeat" is the interval at which a pattern recurs. Large repeats require more yardage. You'll need enough to continue the patterns over seams and to achieve symmetry across a broad expanse.

SOFA & CHAIR SKIRTS

STANDARD TREATMENT
A standard skirt—i.e., the panel of fabric that covers the leg—starts below the apron (the section between the cushion and the base) of the sofa or chair.

WATERFALL TREATMENT
A skirt that starts just below the seat cushion creates a more elongated, graceful look.

KICK-PLEAT DETAILING
Simple pleats at each corner are a classic treatment that works in both modern and traditional settings. For a nice surprise, pick a contrasting fabric for the inside.

SHIRRING DETAILING
A skirt that falls in delicately ruffled shirring is ultra-feminine and brings a dose of shabby chic, but exaggerated ruffles can look too froufrou.

BOX-PLEAT DETAILING
A neat series of box pleats brings well-appointed elegance without being overly feminine. Not for patterned fabrics.

NO SKIRT
Skip the skirt for a cleaner look. Also, pass if your piece is already squat, the legs kick outward past the frame or there are a lot of other skirted pieces in the room.

WELT OPTIONS

WELT VS. NO WELT
Welting (aka piping) is a fabric-covered cord tracing every seam. It imparts a more finished, resolved look. Having no welt is a simpler choice that works in modern settings and in traditional rooms that need toning down.

SELF-WELT VS. CONTRASTING WELT
Welting that matches the upholstery fabric—called self-welt—is the more standard way to go. For graphic pop, choose welting in a different color (contrasting welt) instead.

NAIL HEADS
Tracing the outline of an upholstered piece, nail heads can highlight a shapely frame. Casting a reflective shine like jewelry, the tacks come in various sizes and finishes, from burnished bronze to brazen nickel. Depending on what fabric the tacks are paired with, the result can feel quaintly old-school or a little punk rock.

SLIPCOVERS

Like a dress for your sofa, these fit right over the existing frame (with separate covers for cushions) and can be removed and cleaned, or changed seasonally. One way to liven up a careworn antique, a slipcover hides a multitude of sins: stains, bad upholstery or an overwrought, carved-wood frame. A custom slipcover sized exactly to your piece offers the most elegant tailoring. Use light fabric like cotton or linen, and prewash it (if you have multiple pieces to be covered in the same fabric, wash the fabric together so it fades evenly.)

C.O.M.

An acronym for "customer's own material." When ordering an upholstered piece from a manufacturer, some companies allow you to supply your own fabric (purchased elsewhere), instead of using one of the fabrics that the manufacturer provides. Sometimes there's a small charge for this service. Most upscale brands offer C.O.M., but so do some big retail stores. It's an easy way to customize a standard sofa or chair.

LEG STYLES

TURNED
Articulated turned-wood legs suggest antique pedigree.

BUN FEET
Choose one with carved detail rather than a plain round ball, to add sophistication.

STRAIGHT
The most modern look, tapered wood legs with strong lines have universal appeal.

beds

UPHOLSTERED HEADBOARDS

Headboard shapes range from a simple rectangle to an intricately curved silhouette. While there are many retail upholstered-headboard options, an upholsterer can create almost any shape. Leave the headboard as is, or add definition with welting or nail-head trim. Welting can be the same color as the headboard or a different one. Welting or nail heads can run either right along the edge of the headboard or a few inches in, forming a border. Nail heads tend to make a headboard more masculine.

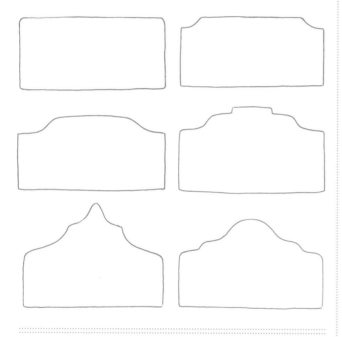

BED SKIRTS

KICK PLEAT
Dressing up the four corners (and sometimes the middle of the long sides), this standard treatment produces a clean, unfussy line.

SHIRRED/RUFFLED
An uninterrupted shirred skirt is romantic and feminine.

BOX
Disciplined box pleats wrap around the base of a bed with classical elegance.

BED HANGINGS

CURTAINS
Straight-hung panels are a nice way to adorn a classic four-poster. Curtains with tie headings are the easiest to hang.

UNSTRUCTURED CANOPY
A draping canopy over the top of a four-poster bed (tied to the corners) gives delicate coverage without bulk.

PELMET WITH CURTAINS
A space-saving decorative pelmet or valance projecting just over the pillow defines a small sheltering nook within a larger room.

CANOPY WITH CURTAINS
Cascading curtains at every corner plus a decorative canopy with pelmet establishes an enclosed aura of intimacy.

PRACTICAL FABRIC CHOICES

HEADBOARDS & BED SKIRTS
For headboards, heavy materials like leather, velvet, wool and canvas in medium to dark colors will stay new-looking longest. With bed skirts, washable fabrics are best—cotton or linen. If going custom (to match the bed skirt with other fabrics in the room), have your fabric prewashed, to ensure that the final product won't shrink when it's laundered later.

throw pillows & trim

THROW-PILLOW SHAPES

SQUARE
Versatile squares are the most popular variety. Mix up a few sizes.

RECTANGLE
The elongated proportions of a rectangular pillow are elegant at a sofa's midpoint, flanked by groupings of square pillows.

BOX
Depth and dimension give a standard square throw pillow more structure.

ROUND
A circular pillow tends to feel retro and plays well against a squared-off seat and back.

ROUND BOX
A round pillow with a few inches of thickness also has retro charm.

BOLSTER
Use these accents on your bed or on both ends of the couch—like armrests.

ANATOMY OF A PILLOW
filler Pillows can have a synthetic filling, be filled with down (the lightest, fluffiest, most expensive feathers), or contain a blend of regular feathers and down. Down is softest but tends to lose its shape, while synthetics hold their form but are stiff. A feather-down blend is moderately priced and holds its shape while still being soft.

closures Both zippers and envelope-style closures allow you to remove the pillow cover for cleaning. Zippers are usually hidden near the seam. Envelope closures are on the back of the pillow and are more casual and less expensive.

TRIMS FOR PILLOWS, CURTAINS & UPHOLSTERY

GIMP
Ribbonlike fabric tape—often ornamented with a braided detail—that smooths over the gap where fabric meets the frame of a chair or sofa.

TAPE
Plain as it is, tape still bestows a couture polish when tracing the edge of a pelmet or sofa.

ROPE
Use rope to add texture and color to the edge of a throw pillow or to make a staid seat cushion more interesting.

RIBBON
Artful, judicious use of ribbon can accentuate the bones of a piece without getting fussy.

POM-POMS
Dangling pom-poms are a sweet touch on demure sofas and chairs. They also fall nicely along the inside edge of curtains.

TASSELS
They bring a sense of movement to furniture and curtains but should be avoided on streamlined pieces because they're so elaborate.

FRINGE
Fringe comes in a multitude of styles. Some, like loop fringe (above), are perfect complements to a well-made curtain in a highly decorated room.

BULLION FRINGE
A cascade of long, weighty, twisted cords works best along the bottom of a heavy curtain or skirted sofa.

THROW-PILLOW DETAILS

WELT: SELF VS. CONTRASTING
On a throw pillow, a welt (or piping) feels finished. Self-welt (in the same fabric as the rest of the pillow) provides the most minimal styling. Or choose an accent fabric/color for definition.

NO WELT/KNIFE EDGE
A knife-edge pillow is one without welting (just a straight seam) and lets patterns wrap around the sides continuously.

FLANGE
A flat-panel border (usually in a solid) encircling a pillow is a way to embellish while still keeping things simple.

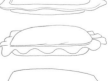

RUFFLE
A voluptuous, ruffled edge is as girly as it gets—even more so in colorful chintz or a bold floral.

TIES
Pillowcases that close with little ties instead of a zipper are quite charming, especially when the outside sleeve contrasts with the fabric inside.

the big black book

a guide to the best decorating resources

resources by category

$ = **AFFORDABLE** $$ = **MID-RANGE** $$$ = **HIGH-END**   X = **NO E-COMMERCE** (BUT PRODUCTS CAN BE VIEWED)

BEDDING

AREA $$
(212) 924-7084; arealinenshop.com
This design studio specializes in cleanly graphic modern bedding that's slightly playful but always sophisticated.

CALVIN KLEIN HOME $$–$$$
(800) 289-6229; macys.com; calvinklein.com/home to view collection
Featuring subtle patterns in a spectrum of neutrals, pastels and earth tones, the mega-designer's linens help build a calming, casually elegant bedroom.

THE COMPANY STORE $
(800) 323-8000; thecompanystore.com
This Wisconsin-based outfit offers a wonderfully comprehensive selection of bedding basics in a wide range of colors, patterns and fabrics.

DONNA KARAN HOME $$–$$$
(866) 593-2540; donnakaran.com
The queen of neutrals' eponymous high-end lines provide subtle colors and textures in luxurious fabrics rich with detail. Her mid-priced Pure DKNY Pure Comfort line references Karan's favorite pieces from her clothing collection.

DWELL STUDIO $$
(212) 219-9343; dwellstudio.com
Truly one-of-a-kind, this New York–based design team turns out colorful, modern interpretations of traditional motifs.

FRETTE $$$
(800) 353-7388; frette.com
Featuring understated design and impeccable materials, the super-luxurious linens from this storied European house are pricey and worth it.

GARNET HILL $
(800) 870-3513; garnethill.com
This well-known catalog brand is an excellent resource for sheets, coverlets and shams. Traditional takes predominate, but there are some more modern styles as well.

JOHN ROBSHAW TEXTILES $$
(212) 594-6006; johnrobshaw.com
The globetrotting designer's printed bedding is one of our absolute favorites. The hand-blocked and hand-printed patterns mix and match beautifully, and the nursery styles are unusually sophisticated.

LEONTINE LINENS $$$ x
New Orleans, Atlanta; (800) 876-4799; leontinelinens.com
Known for standout monograms and fine embellishments, these luxurious handmade linens can be customized to your exact specifications.

MATOUK $$–$$$
(508) 997-3444; neimanmarcus.com; matouk.com to view collection
Family-run since 1929, this old-school American brand now collaborates with modern talents like Lulu DK, but still offers traditional touches like custom colors and monograms.

MATTEO $–$$
(213) 617-2813; matteohome.com
Simple in design but made from luxurious natural materials, this L.A.-made bedding has a modern rustic (but not country) chic.

NANCY KOLTES FINE LINENS $$ x
(212) 219-2271; nancykoltesathome.com
Designed in America and manufactured in Italy, Koltes' traditional silky sheets (including many jacquards and damasks) have an old-world quality and—bonus!—a 14-day return policy. Be sure to check out her cashmere throws.

OLATZ $$$
New York City; (212) 255-8627; olatz.com
A favorite of high-end designers, Olatz Schnabel's super-indulgent linen-and-cotton sheets boast bold color combinations and elaborate hand-embroidered details.

RALPH LAUREN HOME $$$
(888) 475-7674; ralphlaurenhome.com
Nobody does it like Ralph—his sumptuous, tailored bedding has the same timelessness as his clothing, and everything here coordinates effortlessly.

RAWGANIQUE ECO APPAREL LTD. $$
(877) 729-4367; rawganique.com
A favorite for luxury eco-friendly linens, the organic hemp and organic French linen sheets are durable and very luxurious.

SCHWEITZER LINEN $$
New York City; (800) 554-6367; schweitzerlinen.com
For the truly discriminating palate, this New York–based collection offers custom everything alongside a comprehensive collection of well-made basics.

TWINKLE LIVING $
(212) 625-8710; twinkleliving.com
Wenlan Chia's collection of printed sheets and lush throws sports modern florals and dazzling geometric elements.

ENTERTAINING

BARNEYS NEW YORK $$–$$$
(888) 222-7639; barneys.com
This favorite source for luxury goods carries gorgeous Fornasetti platters, elegant servingware and standout pieces by hard-to-find brands like Airedelsur.

BERGDORF GOODMAN $$$
New York City; (800) 558-1855; bergdorfgoodman.com
This Fifth Avenue institution revels in tabletop luxury, offering Kelly Wearstler's sculptural accessories and beautiful wares by Juliska, Varga and William Yeoward, alongside carefully chosen antique objects, including gorgeous silver.

CALVIN KLEIN HOME $$–$$$
(212) 292-9000; macys.com; calvinklein.com/home to view collection
Subtle patterns and atmospheric colors distinguish this top-drawer fashion brand's looks for the table.

GLOBAL TABLE $–$$
New York City; (212) 431-5839;
globaltable.com
Packed with vibrant, unusual items from around the world (all of them simple and graceful, mostly modern in design). This tiny outfit in New York's SoHo is filled with vases, tableware and trays you won't see elsewhere.

JAMALI GARDEN SUPPLIES $
New York City; (212) 244-4025;
jamaligarden.com
This unexpectedly amazing party resource offers strings of lights, floral designers' tools as well as votive candles by the dozen.

MACY'S $–$$$
(800) 289-6229; macys.com
A never-fail purveyor of tasteful fundamentals from Mikasa, Wedgwood and "The Cellar," the store's own line.

MICHAEL C. FINA $$–$$$
New York City; (800) 289-3462;
michaelcfina.com
There's a reason this spot is a favorite for wedding registries; the dazzlingly comprehensive selection of tableware, glassware and serving pieces includes tons of formal and everyday styles.

MOTTAHEDEH $$–$$$
(800) 242-3050; mottahedeh.com
These reproductions of ultra-traditional antique porcelain china are classic, strikingly gorgeous and surprisingly cool.

PEARL RIVER $
New York City; (800) 878-2446;
pearlriver.com
This 35-year-old Chinese department store is the go-to place for all things Asian and crazily inexpensive—ceramic soup bowls and sake sets, chopsticks and paper lanterns in every style and shade.

RALPH LAUREN HOME $$$
(888) 475-7674;
ralphlaurenhome.com
Everything you need to live the Ralph life: a little safari, a little country, all gleaming with old-money swank. The silver-trimmed barware is especially handsome.

SUR LA TABLE $$
(800) 243-0852; surlatable.com
Look for serving pieces and utensils with a slightly rustic, European country feel. We especially like the Jean Dubost cutlery and utensils.

TABLEART $$$
Los Angeles; (323) 653-8278;
tartontheweb.com
The well-traveled owner of this high-end shop marries unexpected, little-known lines from Europe and Asia with marquee brands like Royal Copenhagen and Meissen.

TABULA TUA $$–$$$
Chicago; (773) 525-3500;
tabulatua.com
The inventory at this emporium is truly comprehensive (everyday plates, fine china, serving pieces, vases) and the roster of labels (Juliska, Michael Aram, Ercuis) very impressive.

TAKASHIMAYA $$$
New York City; (800) 753-2038;
takashimaya-ny.com
The stateside outpost of this Japanese department store stocks an elegant East-meets-West collection of artisanal finds. Top picks: flatware and tabletop pieces.

FABRIC AND WALLPAPER (RETAIL)

CALICO CORNERS $
(800) 213-6366; calicocorners.com
The Gap of textile retailers, this national chain with tons of locations and a well-stocked website is a great resource for basic fabrics.

FLORENCE BROADHURST $$$
Los Angeles; (888) 963-5878;
wandrlust.com
We absolutely love the iconic oversize flora and fauna designs by this legendary Australian designer; Woodson & Rummerfield's House of Design in L.A. carries her full line of papers and fabrics.

GRAHAM & BROWN $
(800) 554-0887;
grahambrownus.com
This well-organized online shop makes it easy to browse the house collections and a wide selection of papers by the likes of Marcel Wanders, Barbara Hulanicki and Julien MacDonald.

LES INDIENNES $$$
(520) 881-8122; lesindiennes.com
Created using naturally dyed cottons and traditional hand-blocking methods, Mary Mulcahy's gorgeously subtle, ethnic prints are a wonderful fit in even the most modern interior.

MOD GREEN POD $$ x
(617) 670-2000; modgreenpod.com
Sisters-in-law Nancy and Lisa Mims are the masterminds behind this upstart collection of versatile, Pop Art–influenced textiles in organic cotton.

THE SILK TRADING CO. $–$$ x
(800) 854-0396; silktrading.com
With its huge array of traditional printed and solid textiles and ready-made curtains—much of it in stock—this spot takes the stress out of decorating.

WALNUT WALLPAPER $$$ x
West Hollywood, CA;
(323) 932-9166;
walnutwallpaper.com
Located in Hollywood but with a nicely comprehensive online gallery, this boutique specializes in unique papers by designers including Erica Wakerly and Neisha Crosland.

FABRIC AND WALLPAPER (RETAIL & TRADE)

DE GOURNAY $$$ x
New York City; (212) 564-9750;
degournay.com
The incredibly lush, hand-painted papers here align to create epic historical scenes or grand chinoiserie patterns, but even a single panel can remake a room.

FARROW & BALL $$$
(888) 511-1121; farrow-ball.com
The legendary English manufacturer (famous for its highly pigmented paints) crafts its historic wallpapers with time-tested methods and water-based paints, so that each panel's patterns and tones vary ever so subtly.

FLAVOR PAPER $$$ x
(504) 944-0447;
flavorleague.com
Featuring fire-hydrant toile, Warhol-inspired bananas and

even scratch-and-sniff varieties, everything here is exuberant and statement-making—and hand-printed to order, just in case you want your favorite far-out pattern in a different color.

MARIMEKKO $–$$ x
(800) 656-3587;
marimekkostory.com
Finland's iconic textile and clothing design house continues to turn out bold, bright naif and classic mod prints that are a beautiful fit in any modern interior or ultra-cool kid's room.

NAMA ROCOCO $$$ x
(413) 652-2312; namarococo.com
We're huge fans of this contemporary line's extravagant, slightly funky wallpapers distinguished by their fusion of ornately old-fashioned and very contemporary design. All papers are sold by the sheet.

SEACLOTH $$–$$$ x
Greenwich, CT; (203) 422-6150;
seacloth.com
Filled with motifs plucked from nature, Susan Harris' fabric designs, in a range of saturated colors, are uniformly bright, beachy and happy.

STUDIO PRINTWORKS
$$–$$$ x
(212) 633-6727;
studioprintworks.com
Fanciful, bold and graphic, these fabric and wallpaper designs are rooted in traditional motifs yet wholly modern and almost over-the-top. The company's biggest move of late is a collaboration with renowned American artist Kiki Smith.

TWENTY2 $$–$$$ x
(888) 222-3036; twenty2.net
The Connecticut-based studio creates striking abstract printed papers and coolly geometric textiles in an expansive palette of pop colors.

WAVERLY $$$ x
fabric: (877) 292-8375; wallpaper:
(800) 219-2424; waverly.com
With an archive featuring 25,000 historic fabric patterns, this classic American brand, which launched in 1923, remains an excellent resource for classic designs.

FABRIC AND WALLPAPER (TRADE)

BRUNSCHWIG & FILS $$$ x
(800) 538-1880; brunschwig.com
This firm—more than a century old—is the place to go for authorized repros of Paule Marrot's cheerful florals and Kirk Brummel's contemporary fabrics and papers.

COLE & SON $$–$$$ x
(800) 453-3563; cole-and-son.com
Considerably bolder than you might expect from an outfit that counts the queen as a client, this British company's offerings run the gamut from exuberant nature prints to mod graphics.

COWTAN & TOUT $$–$$$ x
(212) 647-6900; cowtan.com
Old-fashioned and restrained, with shades of English country, the traditional prints here are sold alongside more colorful updates by Manuel Canovas and the girlishly sweet work of Jane Churchill.

DONGHIA $$–$$$ x
(212) 935-3713; donghia.com
Decorators rely on Donghia for beautifully earthy and textured papers and fabrics—we're particularly fond of its fine silks and durable outdoor textiles.

DURALEE $$ x
(800) 275-3872; duralee.com
Great for all of the basics, this is also a good spot to find fun prints just waiting to be discovered and used to transform a fuddy-duddy hand-me-down.

GP & J BAKER $$$ x
(800) 453-3563; gpjbaker.com
Find hundreds of historic and classic English patterns featuring subtle colorations, beautiful small prints and florals. Sprinkled throughout the traditional looks are cut velvets and wovens with a more modern sensibility.

HABLE CONSTRUCTION $$ x
New York City; (212) 228-0814;
hableconstruction.com
Two girls from Texas own this company known for happy, naive-but-not-childish fabrics that strike the perfect medium between fun and sophisticated. A wide selection of the company's ready-made products—including totes, pillows and picture frames—are available online; fabrics are to the trade only.

HINSON & COMPANY $$–$$$ x
(212) 475-4100;
hinsonandcompany.com
The firm of record for the kind of classic American designs—like those of decorating master Albert Hadley and Sister Parish—that will never go out of style.

HOLLAND & SHERRY $$–$$$ x
(212) 355-6241; hollandsherry.com
There's no sorting through hundreds of patterns to get to the good stuff at this well-known rep: Everything is top-notch. Find tons of modern-classic looks from Elizabeth Dow, Winfield and Muriel Brandolini—all tasteful and completely un-granny-ish.

JOHN ROSSELLI & ASSOCIATES $$–$$$ x
(212) 593-2060;
johnroselliassociates.com
Those in the know trust this New York–based dealer for sublime textiles and wall coverings by Robert Kime, Peter Dunham, Seacloth, Carolina Irving and more.

KRAVET $$–$$$ x
(800) 645-9068; kravet.com
The range of fabrics here is pretty dazzling, but it's the basics—simple colors, beautiful textures and timeless styles—that really move us. Look for designer lines by luminaries including Barbara Barry, Windsor Smith and Alexa Hampton.

LEE JOFA $$–$$$ x
(800) 453-3563; leejofa.com
While we love all its luxe printed fabrics and wallpapers, our particular favorite at this established house is the gorgeous array of archival prints.

NEISHA CROSLAND $$–$$$ x
(212) 752-9000; neishacrosland.com
Prints by this London-based designer combine organic motifs with a glam sensibility; her cool circle and oval geometrics are special standouts.

accessing "to the trade" products

WHAT DOES "TO THE TRADE" MEAN?

"To the trade" refers to fabric, wallpaper and furnishings that are available only at showrooms that sell exclusively to decorators, interior designers and architects.

WHAT DOES IT MEAN TO SELL RETAIL AND "TO THE TRADE"?

Some companies that offer "to the trade" discounts to design professionals also sell directly to consumers—at retail prices.

HOW TO BUY TRADE-ONLY PRODUCTS

Decorators and architects have access to every product under the sun; hire one and you will too. But it's also possible to go it alone. Many regional design centers have on-call staff (sometimes decorators) who can make purchases on your behalf from any of the to-the-trade companies listed in this guide, regardless of whether the company has a showroom on site. But you can even do it from home: If you find a fabric or wallpaper you love online or in a magazine, you can call a design service and ask someone there to buy it for you. Either way, you won't get the professionals' discount: You'll pay retail.

REGIONAL BUYING SERVICES

BOSTON
BOSTON DESIGN CENTER
Plush
(877) 767-5874
bostondesign.com

DANIA BEACH, FL
DESIGN CENTER
OF THE AMERICAS
DCOTA Design Services
(800) 573-2682
dcota.com

DENVER
DENVER DESIGN DISTRICT
Design Connection
(303) 733-2455
denverdesign.com

HOUSTON
DECORATIVE CENTER
HOUSTON
Decorative Center Services
(713) 961-1271
decorativecenter.com

LOS ANGELES
PACIFIC DESIGN CENTER
Pacific Design Services
(310) 657-0800
pacificdesigncenter.com

MINNEAPOLIS
INTERNATIONAL
MARKET SQUARE
Design Connection
(612) 338-6250
imsdesignonline.com

NEW YORK
D&D BUILDING
Design Professionals
(212) 759-6894
ddbuilding.com

NEW YORK DESIGN
CENTER
Interior Options
(212) 726-9708
nydc.com

PHILADELPHIA
MARKETPLACE
DESIGN CENTER
Designer Referral Service
(215) 561-5000
marketplacedc.com

SAN FRANCISCO
SAN FRANCISCO DESIGN
CENTER
Access Decor; (415) 565-7115
Buy Design; (415) 626-4944
Just Buy; (415) 626-6689
sfdesigncenter.com

DESIGN SOURCE
(415) 216-7067
designsource-sf.com

SEATTLE
SEATTLE DESIGN
CENTER
The Studio
(206) 762-1200
seattledesigncenter.com

TROY, MI
MICHIGAN DESIGN CENTER
Design Connection
(888) 342-5632
michigandesign.com

WASHINGTON, DC
WASHINGTON DESIGN
CENTER
Dial-A-Designer
(202) 646-6100
dcdesigncenter.com

NATIONAL
L.A. DESIGN
CONCEPTS
(310) 581-3774
ladesignconcepts.com
Online buying service providing a website with direct links to more than 300 "to the trade only" manufacturers.

OSBORNE & LITTLE $$–$$$ x
(212) 751-3333; osborneandlittle.com
A leader in the industry since the 1960s, this London-based company has reissued its debut collection of papers, which range from opulent to proper. Don't miss designer Nina Campbell's historically inspired prints and Designers Guild's colorful patterns.

PHILLIP JEFFRIES LTD. $$$ x
(800) 576-5455; phillipjeffries.com
A company all but synonymous with natural textured wall coverings stocks a rainbow selection of hundreds of grass-cloth papers.

PIERRE FREY $$–$$$ x
(212) 421-0534; pierrefrey.com
This luxury house is so quintessentially French—we love the elegant traditional fabrics and wallpapers, particularly its quirky toiles.

QUADRILLE $$–$$$ x
(201) 792-5959; quadrillefabrics.com
This is the source for the China Seas collection—hand-screened prints that hover between groovily geometric and beach-house boho—and the work of Alan Campbell, whose pop-y graphic designs make a dramatic statement.

RAOUL TEXTILES $$$ x
(310) 657-4931; raoultextiles.com
The color-rich, exotic and occasionally eccentric prints rival those found at an authentic Indian marketplace. The sky's the limit in terms of customization—for a nominal fee, you can have your print of choice custom-colored.

SCALAMANDRÉ $$–$$$ x
(800) 932-4361; scalamandre.com
A favorite for accurate reproductions of historical papers and textiles, as well as a signature line of luxe, antique-inspired contemporary designs.

SCHUMACHER $$$ x
(800) 523-1200; fschumacher.com
This storied American company's designs skew to the classic, but we're also fans of its riskier contemporary design collaborations with notables like Kelly Wearstler and Jamie Drake.

TRAVERS $$$ x
(212) 888-7900
Just the thing for a summer home, Travers fabrics are totally luxurious, with a timelessly preppy, almost tropical sensibility.

FLOORING

CARLISLE WIDE PLANK FLOORS $–$$$ x
(800) 595-9663; wideplankflooring.com
The family business mills wide-plank, heart-pine flooring harvested from a 30,000-acre Alabama plantation, and offers reclaimed products that can all be traced to their structure of origin.

EXQUISITE SURFACES $$–$$$ x
xsurfaces.com
Owner Paula Nataf and her treasure-hunters comb the world for finds, including antique French limestone and French oak, and the company's artisans handcraft beautiful reproductions.

MOHAWK $–$$$ x
(800) 266-4295; mohawkflooring.com
Among the massive crop of flooring solutions from this behemoth, the Handworks line of laminates stands out for its sophisticated parquet and herringbone designs.

PARIS CERAMICS $$$ x
(888) 845-3487; parisceramics.com
Besides vending centuries-old and newly quarried limestone, the in-house design department here can conjure up mosaics, trompe l'oeil patterns and intricate carvings.

SHAW $ x
(800) 441-7429; shawfloors.com
A reliable source for literally thousands of basic, quality wall-to-wall and area options.

FURNITURE

AMERICAN LEATHER $$–$$$ x
(800) 456-9599; americanleather.com
Known for forward-thinking leather pieces, the company also has more classic shapes (including sleeper sofas with solid wood bases replacing the usual metal bars).

BAKER $$$ x
(800) 592-2537; bakerfurniture.com
This classic American company offers an impressive breadth of shapes and styles, all elegant and handsomely tailored; we're particularly fond of the collections by Laura Kirar, Thomas Pheasant and Jacques Garcia and the Baker Studio collection of Scandinavian mid-century modern-esque designs in appropriately pale hues.

BDDW $$$ x
New York City; (212) 625-1230; bddw.com
Score tomorrow's heirlooms today at this large New York showroom, where dramatically rugged and angular handcrafted minimalist wood pieces are built to last.

BERNHARDT $–$$$ x
(866) 451-6314; bernhardt.com
This manufacturer's Martha Stewart collection completely erases shopping anxiety: It's so well designed, you can buy all of it.

BOCONCEPT $–$$ x
(888) 616-3620; boconcept.com
The Danish retailer offers clean, contemporary Scandinavian design, including a wide range of appealingly simple beds, couches, dressers.

CENTURY $$$ x
(800) 852-5552; centuryfurniture.com
We love all the classic styles here, but our very favorite has to be tastemaker Oscar de la Renta's tropical collection of woven outdoor furniture.

CISCO BROS. $$–$$$ x
(323) 778-8612; ciscobrothers.com
The unfussy classic styles hide a green secret: Everything here is built using sustainable wood-and-water-based glues, and manufactured with environmentally friendly processes.

DREXEL HERITAGE $$–$$$ x
(866) 450-3434; drexelheritage.com
The established American furniture maker offers a wide range of styles and collections alongside its newer Postobello Home collection of modernized British Colonial pieces

and the personalizable Mixers line with multiple finishes and hardware options.

ELITE LEATHER $$–$$$ x
eliteleather.com
A new English-inspired line by Nathan Turner (a *domino* contributing editor) and designer Lulu DK's subtly glamorous collection bring some edge to this mostly old-school brand.

ETHAN ALLEN $–$$
(888) 324-3571; ethanallen.com
Though it excels at more traditional pieces (including wood canopy beds in dramatic ebony stains), we also like some of the brand's newer, more modern offerings, like leather sofas and glass-topped desks.

GEORGE SMITH $$$ x
(212) 226-4747; georgesmith.com
Beautifully made, timelessly chic—this is the place to find the upholstered pieces like English-style sofas and ottomans you'll really spend your life with.

GRANGE $$–$$$ x
(800) 472-6431; grange.fr
Hope the grandkids appreciate trad style: These classic European repros are so meticulously made—from the selection of the materials to the application of finishes—they'll be around for generations.

HICKORY CHAIR $$–$$$ x
(800) 349-4579; hickorychair.com
Founded in 1911, this company has built its name with well-crafted, highly traditional pieces destined to be heirlooms. Big-name designer collections include Alexa Hampton and Mariette Himes

Gomez; Thomas O'Brien adds modern pieces to the mix.

JCPENNEY $–$$
(877) 343-3527; jcp.com
Designer Chris Madden's pieces are the biggest draw at this all-American department store, though there are some surprisingly glam finds in the store's mostly traditional house line.

KNOLL $$–$$$ x
(800) 343-5665; knoll.com
Housed in the permanent collections of museums around the world, this manufacturer's modern tables—the sensuous Saarinen, the sculptural Platner, Noguchi's lighthearted "Cyclone"—are sexy design icons.

LANEVENTURE $$–$$$ x
(800) 235-3558; laneventure.com
We trust this North Carolina–based outfit for elegant outdoor wicker furniture; the Celerie Kemble and Mimi & Brooke collections are particular standouts.

**MITCHELL GOLD +
BOB WILLIAMS** $$ x
(800) 789-5401; mgandbw.com
If you thought this beloved company was only about sofas, think again: The constantly updated lighting and accessories collections are every bit as fresh.

NATUZZI $$–$$$ x
(800) 262-9063; natuzzi.com
The epitome of Italian modern design, its signature leather pieces are low, oversize and inviting. The more casual options, created with real life in mind, are perfect for a media room and cozy enough for kids.

OLY $$–$$$ x
(775) 336-2100; olystudio.com
This Berkeley, CA–based company is well loved for its updated riffs on classic French styles and its unique ability to mix antique and contemporary silhouettes.

PALECEK $$–$$$ x
(800) 274-7730; palecek.com
Offering a wide range of furniture made of natural materials—we're big fans of the rattan and bamboo pieces in particular—Palecek is also a pioneer in the world of eco-conscious design.

RALPH LAUREN HOME $$$
(888) 475-7674;
ralphlaurenhome.com
All-American classics dominate the iconic designer's gorgeous home collection, which is as thought-out and timelessly chic as the looks he sends down the runway.

ROOM & BOARD $–$$
(800) 952-8455; roomandboard.com
This popular American retailer offers easy, modern basics for every room in the house, plus outdoor and office styles. Standouts include desks and occasional chairs.

THOMASVILLE $$ x
(800) 225-0265; thomasville.com
More than 100 years after its founding, this company is adding choices—such as a line from decorator Darryl Carter—that reference home and fashion trends but still maintain its traditional, unpretentious roots.

VITRA $$–$$$ x
(212) 463-5750; vitra.com
Since 1950, this company has manufactured furniture for an

incredible range of progressive designers including Charles and Ray Eames, George Nelson, Frank Gehry, Hella Jongerius and Verner Panton.

FURNITURE (RETAIL & TRADE)

LEE INDUSTRIES $$ x
(800) 892-7150; leeindustries.com
All of this eco manufacturer's classic upholstery offerings (slipper chairs, settees, sofas) now adhere to the company's Natural Lee standard, which means soy-based cushions, reclaimed-plastic backs and water-based finishes.

Q COLLECTION $$$ x
New York City; (212) 529-1400;
qcollection.com
The admirable aim of this relatively young furniture company is to deliver chic, traditional designs using only environmentally friendly processes and materials. View the collection online and call the showroom to order.

FURNITURE FOR KIDS

GIGGLE $–$$
(800) 495-8577; giggle.com
This boutique (and its excellent website) is always up on the latest in modern, child-friendly design. We especially like the cribs.

NETTOCOLLECTION $$–$$$
(866) 996-3886; nettocollection.com
Designer David Netto pioneered the concept that children's furniture can be chic—and everything his eponymous studio produces is both truly modern and timelessly stylish.

Q COLLECTION JUNIOR $$–$$$
(212) 529-1400;
qcollectionjunior.com
Made only of wood that's either
FSC certified and/or locally
sourced, these simple, clean-lined
modern designs are finished with
water-based glues, stains, top
coats and paint.

SERENA & LILY $$–$$$
(800) 677-8611; serenaandlily.com
Available at kids' boutiques
nationwide, this contemporary line
has a decidedly traditional bent,
offering everything for the well-
dressed nursery—we especially
love the luxe bedding.

KITCHEN AND BATH CABINETRY

ARMSTRONG CABINETS $ x
(800) 527-5903;
armstrong.com/cabinets
The flooring giant also makes
sturdy, mostly traditional-style
cabinets. Built as modules, they
arrive in a mere 10 to 14 days.

BOFFI $$$ x
(212) 431-8282; boffi.com
For more than 70 years, this
company has issued cutting-edge,
high-modern designs by leading
architects. Slick, minimalist and
beyond functional, the custom
cabinetry here comes in a range of
statement colors.

KRAFTMAID CABINETRY $$ x
(800) 571-1990; kraftmaid.com
One of the first companies to offer
affordable semicustom cabinetry.
The frameless "Venicia" collection
offers a sleek European feel,
with 31 color and finish choices,
including striped Tygris wood.

NYLOFT $$ x
(212) 206-7400; nyloft.net
For high-tech ambience, go to the
sole distributor in the Americas of
Maistri la Cucina kitchen systems,
which feature modern lines in steel,
aluminum and luxe woods.

POGGENPOHL $$$ x
(973) 812-8900 ext. 38;
poggenpohlusa.com
With eye-popping shades and
sleek silhouettes, the world's
oldest kitchen-cabinet brand
seduces like an Italian sports car.
Innovations such as motorized
drawers and eco-friendly water-
based lacquers mean they
perform equally well.

ST. CHARLES CABINETRY $$$ x
(662) 451-1000;
stcharlescabinets.com
This sleek, subtly retro all-metal
cabinetry comes with a pedigree:
It was used by Ludwig Mies van
der Rohe at his iconic Farnsworth
House and by Frank Lloyd Wright
at Falling Water.

KITCHEN AND BATH FIXTURES/ HARDWARE (RETAIL)

DURAVIT $$–$$$ x
(888) 387-2848; duravit.com
Sleekness that doesn't leave
you cold. Top styles: "Vero,"
"2nd Floor" and any of the
Philippe Starck soakers.

ELKAY $$–$$$ x
(630) 572-3192; elkayusa.com
For the high-volume kitchen, the
deep stainless-steel sinks with
tight squared-off corners and flat
sides accommodate pasta pots or
a pile of dishes with aplomb.

FRANKE $$$
(800) 626-5771;
frankeconsumerproducts.com
Designers adore these sturdy
and attractive Swiss-engineered
stainless sinks.

GROHE $$ x
(630) 582-7711; groheamerica.com
Europe's largest faucet
manufacturer specializes in clean-
lined, forward-thinking aesthetics
and technological innovation.

HANSGROHE $$–$$$ x
(800) 488-8199; hansgrohe-usa.com
Solidly built European, fittings,
showerheads and more, ranging
from traditional to hyper-
minimalist. Top style: the whimsical,
high-modern "Axor" line.

KALLISTA $$$ x
(888) 452-5547; kallista.com
A-listers Michael S Smith, Barbara
Barry and Laura Kirar contribute
stunning, mostly traditional
bathware for this high-end
manufacturer.

KOHLER $$–$$$ x
(800) 456-4537; kohler.com
Family-owned since 1873, this
great American concern has
everything—all of it incredibly
well-made.

NEWPORT BRASS $$ x
(866) 417-5207; newportbrass.com
Conscientious decorators rely
on the epic inventory at this
affordable kitchen and bath depot.
Top styles: #920 and #1600 series.

P.E. GUERIN, INC. $$$ x
New York City; (212) 243-5270;
peguerin.com
The handiwork of this venerable
family business—going strong

since 1857—can be seen in
historic homes around the U.S. If
money's no object, indulge in the
painstakingly crafted hardware.

RESTORATION HARDWARE $$
(800) 910-9836;
restorationhardware.com
Solid customer service and
reasonable prices make shopping
Resto's selection very satisfying.
Top styles: "Spritz," "Lugarno"
faucets; "Hutton" washstand.

ROHL $$$ x
(800) 777-9762; rohlhome.com
Artisanal craftsmanship (e.g.,
faucets that riff on Edwardian and
Georgian architecture), plus the
sublime "Modern" line, make this
brand feel older than its 25 years.

**SIMON'S HARDWARE
& BATH** $–$$$
New York City; (888) 274-6667;
simons-hardware.com
This popular Manhattan
showroom contains an impressive
range of hardware and fixtures,
from tiny minimalist hooks to
grand old-fashioned tubs.

ST. THOMAS CREATIONS $$ x
(800) 536-2284;
stthomascreations.com
Clean, substantial, timeless without
being kitschy, this company's
"Richmond" pedestal sink is a
decorator favorite that works in
any style bathroom.

SUNRISE SPECIALTY $–$$ x
(510) 729-7277;
sunrisespecialty.com
This 25-year-old company carefully
crafts authentic reproductions of
Victorian-era bathware, including
a huge range of cast-iron tubs and
faucets, hand showers and tubfills.

URBAN ARCHAEOLOGY
$$–$$ x
New York City; (212) 431-4646;
urbanarchaeology.com
The storied New York destination
offers a well-edited selection
of stylish lighting, hardware,
washstands and freestanding tubs.

WATERWORKS $$$ x
(800) 899-6757; waterworks.com
An established player in the
pricey-but-worth it category. Top
styles: "Belle Epoque," "Palladio"
washstands; "Aero," "Easton,"
"Julia" faucets; "Etoile," "Opus"
showerheads; and any of the
exquisite tubs.

WHITECHAPEL LTD. $
Jackson, WY; (800) 468-5534;
whitechapel-ltd.com
A mind-boggling assortment
of kitchen hardware fills this
impressively organized website,
from reproduction cabinet pulls to
modern hinges to graceful latches.

KITCHEN AND
BATH FIXTURES/
HARDWARE (TRADE
& RETAIL)

E.R. BUTLER & CO. $$$ x
Boston; (617) 722-0230;
erbutler.com
This high-end American
manufacturer lovingly handcrafts
a wide range of traditional and
custom hardware, and produces
designs by such luminaries as Ted
Muehling. Call to find distributors
and showrooms.

THE NANZ COMPANY $$$ x
(212) 367-7000; nanz.com
All of the finely crafted high-end
hinges, knobs and pulls here are

truly beautiful. Though you won't
get the trade discount, you can
research products online and call
the number above to be directed
to a showroom salesperson who
will place your order.

KITCHEN AND
BATH FIXTURES/
HARDWARE (TRADE)

DORNBRACHT $$$ x
(800) 774-1181; dornbracht.com
The rigorously sleek, architectural
hardware for kitchen and bath
from this German manufacturer
never forsakes functionality. Top
style: the super-sultry "Tara" line.
Note: Your contractor can buy this
company's products for you.

KITCHEN AND
BATH TILES

ANN SACKS $$–$$$ x
(800) 278-8453; annsacks.com
One of the biggest names in tile
has everything from basic penny
rounds to collections by designers
Michael S Smith and Angela
Adams; we also like the Sakura line,
inspired by Japanese art.

BISAZZA $$–$$$ x
(800) 247-2992; bisazza.com
The place for Italian glass mosaic,
this adventurous company turns
out high-quality, high-glamour
goods, including an excellent
terrazzo-like glass tile.

COUNTRY FLOORS $–$$$ x
(800) 311-9995; countryfloors.com
Renowned for its European
aesthetic and tiles based on 17th-,
18th- and 19th-century designs,

this L.A.-based company also
showcases beautiful natural-stone
and handmade terra-cotta options.

DALTILE $ x
(800) 449-3592;
daltileproducts.com
Inexpensive ceramic field tiles in
a huge assortment of saturated
hues are conveniently available at
most home-improvement stores.

HEATH CERAMICS $$–$$$ x
Sausalito, CA; (415) 332-3732;
heathceramics.com
Since 1948, this West Coast
establishment has turned out the
distinctive hand-glazed, gently
modern work of groundbreaking
artisan Edith Heath.

SICIS $–$$$ x
New York City; (877) 839-8900;
sicis.com
Feeling a little Liberace? Try this
Italian maverick's fabulously daring
patterns in lavish metallics and
iridescent glass.

LIGHTING (RETAIL)

CHRISTOPHER
SPITZMILLER $$$ x
(212) 563-1144;
christopherspitzmiller.com
Spitzmiller handcrafts modern
lamps with classic influences (such
as the gourd shape) in an array of
colors and silhouettes.

CIRCA LIGHTING $–$$
(877) 762-2323; circalighting.com
With a tremendous stock of floor
and table lamps, sconces and
pendant lights—skewed toward the
traditional, though nothing's too
antique-y—it's no wonder this spot
is so beloved by decorators.

NOVA68 $$
(800) 420-4137; nova68.com
We love this online retailer's vast
inventory—virtually every classic of
modern design is represented here.

REJUVENATION $$
Seattle, Portland, OR;
(888) 401-1900; rejuvenation.com
Besides a strong collection
of antique fixtures and
reproductions, the company has
a take-back program to ensure its
products don't end up in landfills.

SCHOOLHOUSE
ELECTRIC CO. $
Portland, OR; (800) 630-7113;
schoolhouseelectric.com
Past and present merge in this
up-and-comer's wide range of
historically accurate luminaires,
all of which can be hardwired to
order for eco-friendly compact
fluorescent lightbulbs.

YLIGHTING $
(866) 428-9289; ylighting.com
A mega-emporium, with a
massive assortment of modern
options in every category.

LIGHTING
(TRADE)

THE URBAN ELECTRIC CO. $$$ x
(843) 723-8140; urbanelectricco.com
This Charleston-based concern
collaborates closely with top
designers (among them *domino*
favorite Tom Scheerer) on updated
but still timeless options.

VAUGHAN $$$ x
(212) 319-7070; vaughandesigns.com
A wide range of mostly traditional
but unstuffy lights dominates this
British company's repertoire.

RUGS (RETAIL)

ABC CARPET & HOME $$–$$$
New York City; (212) 473-3000;
store.abccarpet.com
This sprawling superstore is
stocked with rare gems like
oversize rugs, unusual antiques
and ethnic pieces from far-
flung locations, alongside new
collections like Madeline Weinrib's.

CHRISTOPHER FARR $$$x
Los Angeles; (310) 967-0064;
christopherfarr.com
In addition to Farr's own Josef
Albers–inspired pieces, the
innovators here carry works by
such designers as Allegra Hicks,
Ilse Crawford and John Pawson.

COMPANY C $–$$
(800) 818-8288; companyc.com
A reliable source for affordable,
brightly colored wovens and
hooked rugs. With prints in
everything from stripes to lobsters,
many would enliven a kid's room.

DASH & ALBERT $–$$x
(800) 442-8157; dashandalbert.com
Shop for amazingly well-priced
colorful patterns plus a big range
of striped and floral options.

EMMA GARDNER DESIGN
$$$x
(877) 377-3144
emmagardnerdesign.com
Gardner turns out gorgeously
hand-worked wool and silk rugs
bearing her trademark eye-
popping whimsical prints.

FLOR $
(866) 281-3567; flor.com
Environmentally responsible
modular carpet tile that installs
faster than wall-to-wall, goes with
you when you move and can be
replaced by section if it gets stained.

JUDY ROSS $$$x
(212) 842-1705; judyrosstextiles.com
Cheerful and graphic, these
organic-modern crewelwork
designs in bright, saturated colors
and earthy neutrals are hand-
embroidered by Indian artisans.

KARASTAN $$x
(800) 234-1120; karastan.com
Known for durable, well-made
reproductions of orientals at
all price levels, this trusted brand
is revamping its image with
modern collections and a super-
helpful website that defuses
oft-intimidating rug searches.

MANSOUR $$$x
Los Angeles; (310) 652-9999;
mansourrug.com
Favored with the Royal Warrant by
H.R.H., the Prince of Wales, these
colossal showrooms (in London
and L.A.) teem with high-high-end
rare antiques from all over the
world, plus Arts and Crafts, Deco
and contemporary styles.

MANSOUR MODERN $$$x
Los Angeles; (310) 652-1121;
mansourmodern.com
The many inventive, ethnic-inspired
patterns at this couture shop are
especially strong, but the range of
designs encompasses everything
from graphic looks (Michael S
Smith's collection is a standout) to
subdued neutrals, all of it striking
and well-crafted.

MERIDA MERIDIAN $$$x
(800) 345-2200;
meridameridian.com
An amazing source for natural
fiber floor coverings like sea grass
and sisal, jute, abaca and beyond,
all beautifully woven and bound
in designs and patterns you won't
see elsewhere.

ODEGARD $$$x
New York City; (800) 670-8836;
odegardinc.com
Company founder Stephanie
Odegard introduced handmade
Tibetan rugs to the U.S. market,
and she continues to offer bold,
inspired designs, while promoting
positive labor practices in Nepal.

THE RUG COMPANY $$$x
New York City, Los Angeles;
(800) 644-3963;
therugcompany.info
Paul Smith, Diane von
Furstenberg, Vivienne Westwood,
Matthew Williamson and other
fashion names are among
the collaborators working to
revolutionize the rug world.

SAFAVIEH $$–$$$x
(866) 422-9070; safavieh.com
More on the traditional, tailored
end of the spectrum, the
selection here includes Thomas
O'Brien's cleaned-up ethnic looks
and Martha Stewart's classically
understated and neutral
collection featuring faux bois and
botanical looks.

RUGS (TRADE)

BEAUVAIS CARPETS $$$x
(212) 688-2265;
beauvaiscarpets.com
As much an art gallery as a
showroom, this spot is dedicated
to fine antique rugs and equally
authentic-feeling reproductions
for the true connoisseur.

COUNTRY SWEDISH $$x
(888) 807-9333;
countryswedish.com
Small patterns including stripes
and diamonds executed in a
handsomely crisp and durable
flatweave are the big draws
at this company known for
its made-to-order traditional
Scandinavian craftmanship.

ELSON & COMPANY $$$x
(800) 944-2858; elsoncompany.com
Handwoven by Tibetan weavers,
the rugs here are far from boho.
This San Francisco company's
stock-in-trade is couture rugs by
such respected names as Oscar
de la Renta and Lulu DK.

KRAVET $$x
(800) 648-5728; kravet.com
A great program here makes
it possible to customize the
color and design of any of the
company's plush, understated
Tibetan rugs. Fans of Michael
Berman and Windsor Smith are
also in luck: These strong graphic
looks can also be dyed to suit.

STARK CARPET $$$x
(212) 752-9000; starkcarpet.com
It's all about the selection and
quality here, from antiques to
repros, Aubussons to soumaks,
and brilliant custom options.

VERMILION $$$x
(212) 593-2060;
johnrosselliassociates.com
For modernists who crave thick,
luxurious, durable floor coverings
(and wouldn't be caught dead
with an Aubusson), this is it.
Choose from stunning options
(including chain-link and Greek
key), and be prepared to sink into
something truly fantastic.

WINDOWS AND DOORS

ANDERSEN WINDOWS $$–$$$ x
(800) 426-4261;
andersenwindows.com
The name is deservedly synonymous with quality; the designs are all built to last, but it's the natural-wood construction and UV light-blocking technology that seal the deal.

JELD-WEN $–$$$ x
(800) 535-3936; jeld-wen.com
This company creates classic designs in whatever material—wood, vinyl or aluminum—suits your particular project. The new accordion-like patio-door system offers streamlined connections between indoors and out.

MARVIN WINDOWS AND DOORS $–$$$ x
(888) 537-7828; marvin.com
A well-kept architect's secret, this is a great substitute for custom. Most of its prices are middle of the road, but the quality and looks are very high-end.

PELLA WINDOWS & DOORS $–$$ x
(888) 847-3552; pella.com
Offering many factory-assembled options that arrive ready to install, this is a good resource for DIY. Bonus: Rustic, handmade Rocky Mountain Hardware is included as an option for many doors.

SMITH + NOBLE $$
(800) 738-0629; smithandnoble.com
The go-to source for window treatments demystifies this complicated subject with well-priced offerings and an easy-to-navigate website.

stores that carry everything

NATIONAL STORES

ANTHROPOLOGIE $$
(800) 309-2500;
anthropologie.com
This favorite has perfected a gently worn bohemian aesthetic that's reflected in everything from elegant sofas to small decorative accessories.

BED BATH & BEYOND $
(800) 462-3966;
bedbathandbeyond.com
A mecca for home essentials, including amazing kitchen basics and exclusive bath accessories and bedding sets by designers like Jonathan Adler.

BLOOMINGDALE'S $$–$$$
(800) 472-0788;
bloomingdales.com
The never-fail purveyor is especially reliable when it comes to tableware (Bernardaud, Kate Spade, Vera Wang) and bedding (everybody from Ralph to Calvin to Donna). Plus, a big selection of furniture.

CONTAINER STORE $–$$
(888) 266-8246; containerstore.com
Every basket and bin you need, plus killer closet-organizing tools and a strong selection of kitchen accessories. Bring in your measurements, and the helpful staff will help you design a custom storage solution.

CRATE & BARREL $$
(800) 967-6696;
crateandbarrel.com
Handsome and solidly built, the mass retailer's furniture looks anything but. A favorite with decorators.

DESIGN WITHIN REACH $$$
(800) 944-2233; dwr.com
One-stop shopping for virtually every modern design classic.

THE HOME DEPOT $
(800) 553-3199; homedepot.com
The renovator's best friend stocks well-priced kitchen and bath fixtures, cabinetry and outdoor essentials.

IKEA $
(877) 345-4532; ikea.com
Though the printed catalog might be easier to navigate than the massive stores, no one does inexpensive, elegantly modern furniture better.

LOWE'S $
(800) 445-6937; lowes.com
With its superior customer service and extensive options, this nationwide chain makes home improvement much less daunting.

PIER 1 IMPORTS $ x
(800) 245-4595; pier1.com
This is the place for basic yet room-finishing accessories like rattan area rugs and tabletop votives and woven baskets.

POTTERY BARN $$
(888) 779-5176; potterybarn.com
These casual, kid-friendly pieces are like comfort food for your home. Favorite pick: the timeless and graceful "Hotel" console.

TARGET $
(800) 591-3869; target.com
Big designers from Thomas O'Brien to Victoria Hagan have done banner collections for this retail giant. Stay tuned for the next new designer rollout.

URBAN OUTFITTERS $
(800) 282-2200; urbanoutfitters.com
Cheery furnishings with a retro-luxe, dorm-room bent. Great for younger apartment dwellers.

WEST ELM $
(888) 922-4119; westelm.com
Modern basics, from perfectly proportioned Parsons tables to classic accent chairs.

WORLD MARKET $
(877) 967-5362; worldmarket.com
These souk-like spaces are packed with handmade furniture and smaller items from exotic locales—all of it very affordable.

CATALOGS ONLINE

BALLARD DESIGNS $$
(800) 536-7551; ballarddesigns.com
An always reliable resource

THE BIG BLACK BOOK

for timeless styles: overstuffed couches, elegant lighting, needlepoint pillows—even adorable monogrammed party supplies.

CB2 $
(800) 606-6252; cb2.com
We love the easy, unfussy modernism here—and the fact that everything is so incredibly priced.

GUMP'S $$
San Francisco; (800) 766-7628; gumps.com
This San Francisco emporium specializes in sophisticated, thoroughly grown-up good design—and the selection is mind-bogglingly comprehensive.

HORCHOW $$
(877) 944-9888; horchow.com
Loaded with carvings and painted insets inspired by Morocco, China and beyond, this family-run establishment's opulent offerings only look as if they cost a fortune.

VIVRE $$–$$$
(800) 411-6515; vivre.com
Find a slew of furniture, accessories and objects from big-name and lesser-known designers, in styles from quirky to glamorous, ethnic to traditional.

WISTERIA $$
(800) 320-9757; wisteria.com
The goods here run the gamut from sofas to votive holders, much of it slightly quirky, and imbued with a globe-trotting, flea-market vibe.

WILLIAMS-SONOMA HOME $$
(888) 922-4108; wshome.com
A reliable source for sophisticated, clean and tailored modern looks.

BOUTIQUES ONLINE

AUTO $$–$$$
New York City; (866) 568-2886; thisisauto.com
From baby clothes to bedding and tablecloths, this nicely curated selection of modern goods is a great destination for gifts.

BELVEDERE $$$ x
Atlanta; (404) 352-1942; belvedereinc.com
Julia-Carr Bayler helped kick-start Atlanta's high-design wave when she opened this vintage-modern store filled with pillows, lamps and ceramics by big names like Dransfield & Ross and Peter Lane.

CHRISTIANE CELLE CALYPSO HOME $$–$$$
(212) 925-6200; calypso-celle.com
The sophisticated ethnic stock (vivid textiles, hammered-silver Moroccan bowls) looks as if it were assembled by a very chic Frenchwoman just back from traveling the globe.

CHARLOTTE MOSS $$–$$$
New York City; (212) 308-3888; charlottemoss.com
High-end designer Moss has turned a landmarked, five-story NYC town house into a country-glam showhouse with a twist: Everything in it—the silver serving pieces, the glassware in the pantry, the luxury linens on the beds—is for sale.

THE CONRAN SHOP $$–$$$
New York City; (866) 755-9079; conranusa.com
The source for nearly every iconic mid-century light fixture, eye-catching contemporary pieces

from Philippe Starck and others, plus great housewares and children's goods.

FRENCH GENERAL $
Hollywood, CA; (323) 462-0818; frenchgeneral.com
An excellent resource for small doses of Gallic chic, like linen hanger covers, organic lavender sachets and a wide range of hard-to-classify oddities and ephemera.

HOLLYHOCK $$$ x
West Hollywood, CA; (310) 777-0100; hollyhockinc.com
Owner Suzanne Rheinstein's 19-year-old shop brings a dose of Upper East Side chic to Melrose, with beautiful traditional antiques from old-fashioned hemstitched napkins to Uzbekistani suzanis.

HUDSON BOSTON $$–$$$ x
Boston; (617) 292-0900; hudsonboston.com
This beautifully curated shop stocks a wide range of furniture (including some vintage treasures) as well as rugs, lighting and smaller accessories, most with a worn-in, preppy New England vibe.

JAYSON HOME & GARDEN $$–$$$
Chicago; (800) 472-1885; jaysonhomeandgarden.com
The superstore has a comprehensive stock of classic furniture and accessories, plus excellent vintage finds and a well-stocked garden section.

JONATHAN ADLER $$
(800) 963-0891; jonathanadler.com
Design entrepreneur and reality-

TV star Adler turns out fun, pop-y yet glamorous rugs, ceramics, lamps, mirrors, furniture, objects and more.

KARKULA $$$ x
New York City; (212) 645-2216; karkula.com
A singular source for striking ultra-modern European and Scandinavian furniture, fine art and elegant tabletop pieces.

LARS BOLANDER $$$ x
New York City, Miami, Palm Beach, FL; (212) 924-1000; larsbolander.com
Pioneering Swedish decorator Bolander's eponymous retail outfit carries a wide array of unfussy Swedish and French antiques and reproductions.

MARSTON & LANGINGER $$
marston-and-langinger.com
Excellent at making the usual unusual, this British home-and-garden store proffers fanciful wire baskets and vases, inventive indoor and outdoor lighting, and elegant throw pillows, along with its signature conservatories.

MATTER $$–$$$
New York City; (877) 862-8837; mattermatters.com
A relative newcomer that's already an institution, Matter offers iconic designs alongside a host of interesting objects, many of them reflecting the store's environmentally and socially conscious stance.

MECOX GARDENS $$$ x
(631) 287-5015; mecoxgardens.com
This mini-chain has seven locations, but the attitude of all the furniure, lighting,

and accessories is distinctly Hamptons-inspired. The outdoor furniture is a standout.

MOMA STORE $$–$$$
New York City; (800) 447-6662; momastore.org
One of the great museum stores, the Museum of Modern Art's shop is packed with modern classics and collectibles, and features an ever-expanding roster of lines (like Japanese mainstay Muji).

MOSS $$$
New York City; (866) 888-6677; mossonline.com
Retail pioneer Murray Moss offers a sophisticated mix of tableware, porcelain, furniture and lighting from an idiosyncratic roster of 20th-century design giants.

PERCH $$
New Orleans; (504) 899-2122; perch-home.com
A New Orleans institution, Perch boasts a huge selection of furniture, textiles, art and accessories, from elegant antiques to cutting-edge contemporary pieces.

PIED NU $$
New Orleans; (504) 899-4118; piednuneworleans.com
Fairly oozing Southern gentility, it offers the chicest selection of furniture in New Orleans.

ROOM SERVICE HOME $$
(800) 588-1170; roomservicehome.com
Filled with pieces big (sofas, dining tables and headboards) and small (vases, lighting and pillows), all of it comfortable and relaxed in styles from mid-century modern to Hollywood Regency.

RUBY BEETS $$$ x
Sag Harbor, NY; (631) 899-3275; rubybeets.com
New and vintage stock here includes farmhouse tables, metal baskets, muslin-upholstered George Sherlock sofas and Serge Mouille lamps. Ideal for finishing touches like wood-framed mirrors and simple oil paintings.

TREILLAGE $$–$$$ x
New York City; (212) 535-2288; treillageonline.com
A joint venture of designer Bunny Williams and antiques dealer John Rosselli, this store has dramatic new and antique pots, planters and finials, as well as indoor pieces like gorgeous hurricane lamps and fantastic trimmed pillows.

VELOCITY ART AND DESIGN $$
Seattle; (866) 781-9494; velocityartanddesign.com
Here you'll find a comprehensive—though well-edited—roster of playful modern classics; we especially like the selection of seating and serving pieces.

Z GALLERIE $
(800) 908-6748; zgallerie.com
Find a wild mix of pieces—both playful and stately—from around the globe.

ANTIQUES ONLINE

1STDIBS.COM $$–$$$
Decorators rely on this dream resource filled with high-quality antiques and new items culled from some of the finest shops and showrooms in the U.S., France and England, all vetted

by owner Michael Bruno's discriminating eye.

ARTNET.COM $$$
(800) 427-8638
Best known as a one-stop info shop for fine-art galleries and auctions worldwide, the super-searchable site also boasts a substantial "design marketplace," in which readers can browse top-shelf 20th and 21st-century wares from Steuben to Saarinen—and find out where to buy them.

RUBYLANE.COM $–$$$
A huge clearinghouse for antiques, collectibles, art and jewelry that features almost 2,000 independent online stores, each prescreened by the site's own pros.

worth a visit…

ABC CARPET & HOME $$–$$$ x
New York City; (212) 473-3000; abchome.com
With the exception of rugs (for sale at store.abccarpet.com) there's no online shopping at this one-of-a-kind Manhattan mega-emporium stocked with treasures old and new (many of them eco-friendly) from the most remote points on the globe. Look for the world's comfiest sofas and a well-vetted bedding selection.

H.D. BUTTERCUP $$–$$$ x
Los Angeles; (310) 558-8900; hdbuttercup.com
Its website is not much more than a marquee, but this unique concept fills the gap between big-box stores and exclusive design centers. Housed in an enormous Art Deco building in

Culver City, more than 50 top furniture manufacturers offer everything from oriental carpets to luxury mattresses, without the usual middlemen.

JOHN DERIAN COMPANY $$ x
New York City, Provincetown, MA; (212) 677-3917; johnderian.com
While the website gives only a taste of this store's offerings, we had to include this because it is one of our favorite decorating and gift shops. All of the designer's découpaged pieces (plates, lamps and more) and an assemblage of French ceramics, Indian linens and upholstered furniture share the same slightly dark, Victorian feel.

acknowledgements

a big thank-you

To Sarah Min for wrestling this book out of our
hands and into print—without her, there
would be no *domino: The Book of Decorating*

To Stella Bugbee for her leadership, grace
and unerring design sensibility

To Ruth Altchek and Deb Schwartz, who wildly
exceeded the totally unreasonable demands
placed on them, and with charm and humor to boot

To Danielle Claro, Lia Ronnen and our
editors at Simon & Schuster,
David Rosenthal and Amanda Murray,
who nurtured this project from the beginning.

TO THE BRILLIANT PEOPLE
IN AND AROUND *DOMINO*
WHO CONTRIBUTED TO THIS BOOK

Melanie Acevedo, Rumaan Alan, Lisa Ano, Kristin Auble, Monika Biegler Eyers,
Kate Bolick, Grace Bonney, Chase Booth, Tom Borgese,
Beth Brenner, Elizabeth Brownfield, Missy Bruggeman, Susannah Kraft Butscher,
Alyson Cameron, Andrew Carbone, Jennifer Condon, Paul Costello,
Billy Cotton, Bridget Dearborn, Tom Delavan, Lili Diallo,
Cindy DiPrima, Kate Doherty, Rebecca Donnelly, Kate Donovan,
Lucilla Eschmann, Julia Felsenthal, Kim Ficaro,
Hilary Fitzgibbons, Miguel Flores-Vianna, Kim France,
Lucy Gilmour, Lauren Goodman, Ruth Graham, Alison Griffin,
Lisa Guernsey, Allison Gumbel, Catherine Halley, Mary Alice Haney,
Kirsten Hilgendorf, Shelley Jefferson, Victoria Jones, Jenny Kim,
Max Kim-Bee, Cynthia Kling, Rita Konig, Katie Levine, Isaac Lubow, Yarrow Lutz,
Stacie McCormick, Marian McEvoy, Clio McNicholl,
Tori Mellott, Olga Naiman, Joni Noe, Nick Olsen, Rebecca Omweg,
Stephen Orr, Nicolette Owen, Amy Peck, Chris Penberthy,
Chassie Post, Jen Renzi, Michelle Rubel, Christine Rudolph,
Eugenia Santiesteban, Allison Sarofim, Jeff Schad,
Sophie Schulte-Hillen, Robin Sillau, Emily Slaughter, Ariana Speyer,
Sunny Stafford, Allison Tick, Kate Townsend,
Stephen Treffinger, Nathan Turner, Lesley Unruh, Gretchen Vitamvas,
Brooke Williams, Bess Yoham, Macon York, Zoë Wolff, Alexandra Sanidad Zangrillo

TO OUR BOSSES FOR MAKING *DOMINO* POSSIBLE

S.I. Newhouse Jr., Charles Townsend, Tom Wallace, Rick Levine

TO OUR FAMILIES FOR MAKING EVERYTHING POSSIBLE

Jacob, Lily and Nathaniel Weisberg
Paul, Harrison and Carolina Costello
David, Sofia and Stefan Steinberger

xoxo, Deborah, Sara and Dara

more big thanks

TO THE HOMEOWNERS AND DESIGNERS WHO OPENED THEIR
DOORS—AND WHO INSPIRE OUR WORK

Jonathan Adler

Virginia Apple

Kimberly Ayres

Michael Bargo

Sara Bengur

Barrie &
Matt Benson

Nate Berkus

Barbara Bestor

Elizabeth Blitzer

Sheila Bridges

Anita Calero

Nina Campbell

Haylynn Cohen

Eric Cohler

Cristi Conaway

Natascha Couvreur

Ilse Crawford

Gray Davis

James Leland Day

Cloud Devine &
Laura Resen

Peter Dunham

Ashley Edwards

Stephen Elrod

Tripp Evans

Krista Ewart

Erin Fetherston

Vesta Fort

Fawn Galli

Steven Gambrel &
Chris Connor

Meghan Gerety &
Michael Phelan

Tori Golub

Albert Hadley

Austin Harrelson

Johnson Hartig

Carolina Herrera Jr.

Allegra Hicks

India Hicks

Ames Ingham

Carolina Irving

Katie Lee Joel

Jenni Kayne

Liz Lange

Celerie Kemble

Delphine Krakoff

Marisa Leichtling

Christian Liaigre

Katie Lydon

Lily Maddock

Lisa Mahar

David Mann

Jenna Lyons Mazeau &
Vincent Mazeau

Annsley McAleer

Mary McDonald

Mary McGee

Will Meyer

Charlotte Moss

Adrienne Neff

David Netto

Thomas O'Brien

Frouwkje &
Stéphane Pagani

Lisa Perry

Mary Jane Pool

Laura Vinroot Poole

Jessie Randall

Miles Redd

Serena Rees

Suzanne Rheinstein

Markham Roberts

Kelly Rutherford

Schuyler Samperton

Michelle & Derek Sanders

Ahmad Sardar-Afkhami

Gil Schafer

Tom Scheerer

Carina Schott

Suze Yalof Schwartz

Suzanne &
Christopher Sharp

Sarah Shetter

Stephen Shubel

Kari Sigerson

Sharon Simonaire

Ione Skye

Windsor Smith

Ruthie Sommers

Estee Stanley

Matthew Sudock

Alice Temperley

The Apartment

Laurie Thiel

Antony Todd

Benjamin Trigano

Camilla Trigano

Chloe Warner

Timothy Whealon

Ashley Whittaker

Vicente Wolf

Lucy Wrubel

Laura Yaggy

269

fabric & wallpaper credits

cover
DE GOURNAY
"Portobello"
#541141
wallpaper in
Blue Gray
degournay.com

p.6
COLE & SON
"Malabar-W"
#66/1006 wallpaper
in Pale Blue and
White
cole-and-son.com

p.10
SCHUMACHER
"Vallier Vine"
#173771 fabric in
Graphite, Matthew
Patrick Smyth
Collection for
Schumacher
fschumacher.com

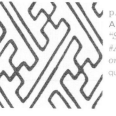

p.24
ALAN CAMPBELL
"Saya Gata"
#AC207-45 in Blue
on tinted linen
quadrillefabrics.com

p.50
FARROW & BALL
"Plain Stripe"
#ST 1704 wallpaper
in Grisaille
farrow-ball.com

p.82
OSBORNE
& LITTLE
"Sabai" #F974/07
fabric
osborneandlittle.com

p.108
MANUEL
CANOVAS
"Treillis" #3021-07
wallpaper in
Citrine
cowtan.com

p.134
LEE JOFA
"Althea"
#879001-LJ
fabric in Beige,
Leafgreen on
Ivory
leejofa.com

p.162
BOB COLLINS
"Lotus Dynasty"
#KB.V.202 fabric
in Peach and
Turquoise
(800) 282-9971

p.186
TRAVERS
"Grammont"
linen #107133
in Chestnut/
Champagne
(212) 888-7900

p.212
HINSON
& COMPANY
"Trixie" #HP-1003-R
wallpaper in Red/
Black on White
(212) 475-4100

p.238
BRUNSCHWIG
& FILS
"Island
Taffeta Stripe"
#89302.01/440
fabric in Ivy
brunschwig.com

p.250
HINSON & COMPANY
"Coarse Madagascar-
Unbacked"
#HY-0390-AU
wallpaper
(212) 475-4100

p.264
GP & J BAKER
#158408C fabric in
#R1375-3 color
gpjbaker.com

photography credits

ABRANOWICZ, WILLIAM
41, 76, 97, 151, 177, 201, 205

ACEVEDO, MELANIE
14-15, 20-21, 37, 66, 67, 69, 71,
73, 75, 78, 80, 94, 97, 99, 128,
140-141, 151, 153, 157, 164-165,
166-167, 179, 192-193, 201, 207,
216-217, 227, 229, 231, 233

ACHILLEOS, ANTONIS
45, 127

ALBIANI, MATT
36, 126, 155

ALLEN, LUCAS
26-27, 39, 69, 71

ARNAUD, MICHEL
103

BELLO, ROLAND
46

BERNHAUT, JUSTIN
43, 95, 101, 123, 155, 203, 229

BLACK, DAVID
79, 157

CAHAN, ERIC
56-57, 101, 178, 205

CALERO, ANITA
180

CARTER, EARL
64, 67

CORONA, LIVIA
103

COSTELLO, PAUL
14-15, 30-31, 40, 41, 52-53, 58-59,
67, 72, 77, 78, 99, 102, 103, 120,
123, 125, 129, 130, 131, 132-133,
142-143, 148, 149, 151, 155, 157,
158, 160-161, 168-169, 174, 177,
179, 181, 182, 184-185, 188-189,
199, 200, 201, 214-215, 224, 227,
228, 229

DEVINE, CLOUD
43

DIRAND, JACQUES
43 (top right, home of Christian
Liaigre), 54-55, 68, 198

DISCHINGER, FRANÇOIS
39

DONNE, TARA
175

ESTERSOHN, PIETER
125

FLORES-VIANNA, MIGUEL
39, 41, 74, 75, 86-87, 101, 121,
154, 156

FREEMAN, DON
45, 65

FRIEDMAN, DOUGLAS
73, 97, 100, 123, 124, 127, 157,
202, 231

GRUEN, JOHN
155

HRANEK, MATTHEW
71, 152, 225, 232

ISAGER, DITTE
129, 199

JAFFE, DEBORAH
18, 19, 69

KIM-BEE, MAX
65, 136-137, 150, 190-191, 203,
204, 207, 208, 210-211, 226

KVALSVIK, ERIK
174

LAGNESE, FRANCESCO
39, 45, 71, 181, 203

McHUGH, JOSHUA
121, 125, 175

MERRELL, JAMES
36, 43, 44, 129, 151

MOORE, ANGELA
28-29

MOSS, LAURA
127

MUNRO, SOPHIE
64, 70

OTSEA, ERIK
103

PENNEY, JASON
198

RESEN, LAURA
84-85, 88-89, 94, 96, 99,
114-115, 153, 225, 227, 229

ROWLEY, ALEXANDRA
122

SAMUELSON, JEREMY
231

SCHLECHTER, ANNIE
42, 46, 48-49, 73, 104,
106-107, 120, 127, 205, 231,
234-235, 236-237

SLERTMAN, MILLA
21

UNRUH, LESLEY
79

UPTON, SIMON
37, 75, 101, 112-113,
138-139, 149, 153, 176, 177,
181, 206, 207, 218-219, 224,
227, 233

VANG, MIKKEL
41, 77, 78, 80-81, 95, 203

WADDELL, JAMES
20-21, 38, 98, 110-111, 177,
179, 230

WALTER, COREY
67, 69

WATSON, SIMON
99, 125

WOLF, ANNA
75, 207

EDITED BY
Danielle Claro,
Ruth Altchek & Deb Schwartz

DESIGN DIRECTION
Stella Bugbee

DESIGN BY
James Casey

CHAPTER OPENERS & FURNITURE ILLUSTRATIONS
James Noel Smith

FLOOR-PLAN ILLUSTRATIONS
Matthew Caserta

HANDBOOK ILLUSTRATIONS
Frank Santoro

PRODUCED BY

Melcher Media, Inc., 124 W. 13th St., New York, NY

Charles Melcher, Publisher
Bonnie Eldon, Associate Publisher
Duncan Bock, Editor in Chief
Lia Ronnen, Executive Editor
Coco Joly & Daniel del Valle, Editorial Assistants
Jessi Rymill, Production Artist
Kurt Andrews, Production Director

This book was typeset in *domino* Clarendon,
domino News and *domino* Stymie.